An old legend about man and dog tells of the creation of the world and of a great rift that opened in the earth. On one side of the rift stood all the four-legged animals. On the other side, man stood alone.

Among the animals was the dog. The dog watched as the rift slowly widened. Suddenly he made a mighty leap. It carried him toward the far side where man stood. His front paws caught the edge. Man bent down and pulled him up. Man and dog stood together, separated from all other animals. The dog has ever since remained at man's side, a faithful, loving, friend.

Like many legends this one tells something important: The dog has chosen man in a way that no other animal has. Your dog gives you his heart. He is happiest when he is with you. He wishes to please you. He will protect you with his life.

TO: Odie's Parents
Jennifer & Duncan

This book is about love, pure + simple & you found it in your dog.

I'm so happy for you!

Love,

From The Story Of Dogs, the Origin and History of Man's Best Friend *by Patricia Laube*

Jetta's Journey

by
Denise Solters

Oak Tree Press   Taylorville, IL

Oak Tree Press

Oak Tree Press books may be purchased for educational, business or sales promotional purposes. Contact Publisher for quantity discounts.

First Edition, September 2010

10 9 8 7 6 5 4 3 2 1

Cover by MickADesign.com

Illustrations by Isobel Hoffman
Author Photography by Karen McClain

ISBN 978-1-892343-72-7
LCCN 2010933220

Dedication

I dedicate this book in loving memory of my father, Harry Francis Came. The finest part of him lives on in me—his love of nature and dogs. I believe Dad is in heaven with his two beloved boxers, Sinbad and Fritz, his energetic dogs who introduced me to dog slobber. We shared crawling space and they let me eat table scraps out of their dog dishes. I formed a bond with man's best friend that has been a powerful force and passion all my life. Dad will remain in my heart forever; I'm grateful that he witnessed the miracle of creating a working dog. He loved Jetta.

This is also dedicated to the people who changed my life—Matthew, my son, who was my reason for living; his loving, beautiful wife, Jennifer, who gave him a reason for living and two beautiful babies: Hudson, who melts my heart; and Rylie, who will give her father love that only a daughter can give; and Jeremy, the best big brother they could have. I also dedicate this to my wonderful goddaughter and niece, Mora Denise, who lets me love her as my own.

Table of Contents

Dedication v

Butterscotch Eyes ix

Prelude xi

Chapters:

Puppy in Training 1

Shopping Day 3

Kitty Street 7

First Time at the Beach 9

First Sleepover 11

Farmer's Market Final Exam 13

Canine Good Citizen Test 15

Visit to Luke 17

Bath Time 19

Lifeguard Jetta 21

Search for the Perfect Ball 23

Day at the Beach 25

Aquanetics Jetta 29

Jetta's Great Escape 31

Birthday Party 33

Therapy Dog 37

Hershey's Last Goodbye 39

Jetta Gets Her Kitty 41

Cookie Monster 45

Jetta's Great Embarrassment 47

Mom Goes to the Hospital 49

Jetta Goes to College 51

Jetta Goes to Kindergarten 55

Jetta Meets a Fireman 59

Visit to Hansel's and Gretel's House 61

Working Day 65

Halloween Hospital 69

Scooter Mom 73

Jetta's Lunch Date 77

Grandpa's Last Goodbye 79

Lumps and Bumps 81

Mom's Other Job 83

Jetta's Lazy Pazy Days 87

When I Am An Old Dog 91

Acknowledgements 93

Butterscotch Eyes

When I saw Jetta, my new puppy, for the first time, she was a ball of energy, running on clumsy black puppy feet, hips wiggling like a hula girl, tail wagging fast like a pendulum. She ran almost sideways, bounding toward me with joy to offer sweet, wet kisses. Jetta would be my first Service Dog. When I looked into her butterscotch eyes that gazed into my soul, I knew I'd found a partner for life.

A piece of my heart was empty until Jetta came into it. Unable to have a dog for many years after my brain injury, I prayed for a dog. I knew the timing was right when I first heard about Jetta. A dog trainer told me that a litter of puppies was due. Big, sweet, gentle and smart, the mother was everything I hoped for in a dog. The breeding and temperament of her pups would be ideal for me, and one of her pups would be just right. I chose Jetta just after she was born.

We loved each other from the first moment, a perfect fit, and we have taken care of each other ever since. Her beauty is breathtaking. She struts her stuff and does the hula for people she meets on our daily beach walks. She does her sideways run and people stop in their tracks, delighted by her grace and gentle, loving spirit. Attracting people like a magnet, she invites folks to play ball by trotting up and dropping the ball at their feet, gazing at them with her butterscotch eyes. They fall in love with her, too.

Sensitive to children and unhappy individuals, Jetta has a unique ability to nurture them. I have watched her with a frightened child, and before I know it, they are rolling around on the floor together, being silly. She draws the best out of people and makes everyone happy. People melt like butter when Jetta looks at them.

Now I never walk the beach alone. Every day with Jetta is a blessing. I still can't take my eyes from her coal-black velvet coat and those butterscotch eyes that gaze into my soul.

Prelude

I was born to be a Service Dog. Lynn, my breeder, tells me I am the pick of my litter. I will grow big and strong like my dad, and friendly and loving like my mom. I will be perfect for my special job, helping a disabled woman named Denise to walk safely. My training will take two years and I will have to pass a test before I will be a real Service Dog. I must learn how to walk nicely on a leash next to Denise, pick up items she drops, get the telephone when it rings, and help Denise stand up when she falls.

I have eight brothers and sisters. Some are yellow, like Mom, and some are black like Dad and me. I like playing with them, and I like chomping on houseplants, too. But Lynn tells me, "No," and I stop chomping. I love to carry something in my mouth—a bone, a ball, or treats. I want to be a good girl.

"Jetta, come here, girl."

That must be my name. I like it.

CHAPTER 1

Puppy in Training

Now I am ten weeks old. I move to a ranch to work with a special dog trainer named Mette.

Mette learned how to train Service Dogs at Canine Companions for Independence in Santa Rosa, California. Usually she starts training dogs when they are two to three years old, but Mom convinced her to start me off on my Service-Dog training as a puppy. Mette and Mom agreed that if I don't learn all that I need to, I cannot be her Service Dog. I don't want to disappoint either of them. I am smart and a fast learner. I will love having a job.

At Mette's ranch, Denise visits twice a week. I love to play with her. She brings me yummy treats.

Mette says, "No jumping on Denise."

I try to remember that. If I pull too hard on the leash, I could hurt her. I don't have any manners yet. Mette says, "Practice, practice, practice." There sure is a lot for a puppy to remember.

Mette smells great—horse, dog, cat and pony aromas. I sniff her for hours. When we go in public, I wear a pretty scarf that has "Service Dog" on it so people will know I'm a puppy in training. I am learning how to help Denise. Mette knows the way to my heart is with food. She makes interesting treats for rewards—tiny hot dog pieces, chunks of cheese, and bits of kitty food. I love kitty food. It's like candy to me. I'm learning commands like sit, come, and stay. Mette rewards me when I listen and obey. Easy! I'm such a good girl.

Mette's ranch has acres of great smelling shrubs and plants, a pony, and a horse. Three other dogs form my new pack. Mette's big, friendly dog, Rover, likes to roam. Fido is a grouchy, scruffy old dog. I sniff near his food, and he growls and bites me on my pretty nose. He makes me cry. Not nice. Tinker, who is a trainee too, looks like me, but is smaller. Sweet and shy, she is learning to help a lady in a wheelchair. Tinker is a good girl like me. She is my best friend.

A horrible black cat hisses and tries to jump on me. Danger, bad kitty. I have to move fast. He has got to go. I get in trouble when Mette sees me chase the little Siamese scaredy cat, but it is so fun. Mette says, "No chase kitty." Sometimes I forget. Sometimes I just do what puppies do, but I am still a good girl.

I love sniffing around the stables. I find interesting smells to roll in. Mette's horse looks down at me, whinnies, and tries to kick my adorable self. Not good. Mette's horse couldn't care less about this cute puppy.

Rover finds a hole in the fence and squeezes through. Should I follow? Tinker is afraid to go, and old Fido is napping in the warm sun. I don't know if I should follow Rover, Hmm— I think it will be okay. Putting my nose to the ground, I follow Rover down the dusty dirt road that leads to town. A rabbit runs and darts in and out of the bushes. He is so fast. We have to chase him. Down a hole he goes. We dig. I feel so wild! I love digging; Rover does, too.

Rover takes me to the lake and wants me to swim with him. I don't know if I should. I'm nervous. I have never been swimming. I wade in and take a long, cool drink.

Rover loves the water. I swim to him, but I am just a puppy. I am tired, cold, and hungry. I feel like whining.

It is getting dark when I hear a truck. Is it Mette's? I hope so. I hear Mette's whistle. We are in trouble. Mette does not look happy to see us so dirty and wet. She was worried about me. I love Mette; she is a great pack leader. I lick her face. I am a good girl.

I am meant to be a working Service Dog. Mette hopes I will pass the training and tests, but Denise already knows I have a brave heart and will spend my life helping her. She's my new Mom. We have a bond of love.

CHAPTER 2

Shopping Day

Today is an important day in my training. I am five months old now. Mom and Mette and I will meet at my favorite grocery store for training. Mette will watch me to see if my new mom and I will be safe together.

Since puppies in training learn better when they have playtime before working, Mom and I go first to the dog park, a place with plenty of dogs to sniff and play chase games with me. I get tired from playtime and hungry, too!

Once I have played, I have to work. Before we meet Mette at a grocery store for our training session, Mom says, "Get dressed." I come close and lower my head so she can put on my working scarf. "Service Dog" is embroidered on it so people will know I am on the job.

When we arrive at the store, Mette is already there to watch us work as a team. "Out" means I need to get out of the car. First I need to stretch.

Mom says, "Let's go."

Oh, no. Mom dropped her keys and needs me to pick them up. I don't like metal in my mouth, but I'll do it for a treat. Ick! I am such a good girl.

We walk into the grocery store. I watch the sliding doors. I know to tuck my tail. Those doors move fast. Inside the store, people, carts and children move around me. I need to focus. I love kids, but I can't be petted until Mom says I can. I have to put my head down and not wag my tail when people talk to me or touch me. Why don't parents tell their children I'm on duty? This is the hardest part of my job. I have to be such a good girl or Mom could get hurt.

The smells in this store have me on food alert. My mouth waters. I can hardly keep my nose from sniffing everywhere. This store smells like heaven.

Look, Mom, free food samples. This is my favorite section in the market. What's on the platter? Pumpkin pie with whipped cream. The nice lady wants to give me food. Well, I tried to stay. Oh, so tasty. Mom, can I sit here and keep her company while you shop? She loves feeding me. I'll lick crumbs off the floor to help clean up like I do at home. I'm a good girl.

Food is on the floor. Nose alarm. I want to vacuum with my mouth.

Mom says, "Leave it."

I had better not eat those bits of crackers on the floor. Mette is watching us from down the aisle. I have to be good. I am a good girl.

Cheese department. This is my favorite section in the market. Oh no. I am drooling all over. There is a slimy puddle where I stand. Be careful, Mom, wet floor. Watch your step. Oh good, the man is wiping it up. How embarrasing.

A child is hanging on to me. What do I do now, Mom? I can't ignore her. Her sticky pudding fingers and face need licking. Jetta's Face-Cleaning Machine is at your service. I love children. They are at my level. Thank goodness, Mom says "Release" and puts me off duty.

Back on duty, and Mom dropped her sunglasses. I'll get them for her. I am a good girl.

I see my friendly butcher. His apron smells divine. His shoes, too. I want to stand next to him and sniff his apron. This meat section is my favorite part of the store. When I'm working, it's hard not to sniff. Mom puts me off duty, so I can smell him. I wish he could come home with us. He gives the best bones. I love him.

Oh! I see a tennis ball coming right at me. Mette is testing me. I want to get the ball. Is it playtime? Mom said, "Leave it." I have to let the ball go rolling down the aisle.

I am fast enough to still get it. Another ball is headed my way. What to do, what to do? This is hard for me. I really want to play. I won't go for the ball. I'll sit here and let the ball go past me. I am a very good girl.

We have been shopping for such a long time. We turn into the pet-food aisle. This is my favorite section in the store. Look, Mom, this big rawhide just popped into my mouth. Can I keep it? It has my drool all over it. All right! She put it in the cart. We pass my favorite peanut-butter cookies for dogs. I'll stop right in front of them and give her my pitiful, sad face. She put some in her shopping cart. Thump, thump, thump. My tail is happy. Mom is such a good girl.

Mom says my favorite word: "Release."

As a special treat for such a good training session, Mom opens the box of dog cookies. I feast on one. So good. People gather around me to watch. I love meeting new people. They pet me and give me hip massages and belly rubs. I flop on the floor and enjoy the attention. Mette says it's an important part of my socialization. Service dogs must be friendly and loving with everyone. After all, I am still a puppy in training. Mom and Mette are pleased with my session today. Now we get to play at the lake. Yippee! I am such a good girl.

CHAPTER 3

Kitty Street

I love to play the chase game with kitties. I love to make them run fast, fast, fast. Their little legs move so fast, and their little good-to-sniff bottoms scoot, scoot, scoot along the ground. Mette's nasty big black kitty hisses at me and makes me afraid. Her scaredy Siamese kitty runs and hides. I'm still just a silly six-month-old puppy; it's my nature to chase kitties.

My new mom, Denise, is meeting Mette and me for more training. I still live with Mette on her ranch. We train a lot. I wonder what lessons we will practice today? I love working when I am rewarded with treats. Mette says I am food motivated, whatever that means. I sure like to eat. Mom gets out of her car and Mette gives her my leash. First, I must greet her and lick her face. I love my new mom.

Where are we? I don't remember this place. I see kitties, a lot of kitties. Where did they all come from? I want to run and chase.

Mom says," Leave it. Leave it."

I see kitties in the street and kitties on porches; I see kitties hiding in bushes and high in the trees. I see kitties on cars and kitties lying on the sidewalk, snoozing in the morning sun. I don't think they want to move for a puppy in training. Now I walk slow and nice for Mom.

She says, "Let's go."

That means she wants me to walk on her left side. How can this be? I can't think with all these fluffy kitties in my path. Mette is testing me to be a good Service Dog. I want to chase, but it is not allowed if I want to be with Mom all the time. I just lower my head and walk by. No sniffing allowed either. Bummer.

I made it across one-half of the sidewalk, but a big, fat, white kitty is sunning her fat self on the other side.

"Excuse us," Mom says.

I step over the kitty. I have never done that before. I am so excited my tail wags fast in circles and my ears stick up with excitement. I want to sniff and chase. She is so close, one little sniff wouldn't hurt.

"Leave it."

I know. If I want to be a Service Dog, I have to "Leave it" like Mom says. I can't do this, Mom. It's hard to "No chase kitties." We walk up and down the street again and again. That one big kitty hisses at me and scares me.

Now Mom says I have to walk in a circle. "Down."

Oh, no. That means lying down at kitty-eye level. That hissing cat is pretty horrible. Are you sure you want to make me do this, Mom?

"Down, Jetta."

She means business. I must lie down in agony at kitty-eye level. That means the cat is the boss. I put my life in danger for you, Mom.

"Okay. Jetta, what a good girl you are! I am so proud of you. You will be a great Service Dog when you are all grown up," Mom tells me.

I have to grow up knowing that kitties are "No chase." I know I can do this because my new mom would be so sad without me in her life. I want to be her Service Dog, so right now I don't care if I ever chase a kitty again. At least not today. Maybe tomorrow. Puppies in training have to have some fun. I'm such a good girl.

CHAPTER 4

First Time at the Beach

My new mom is picking me up today at Mette's ranch to take me to her beach. I will be a good girl and sleep in Mom's car for the long trip. Mette, my trainer, likes me to be a quiet traveler. I'm in training to be a Service Dog. I'm seven months old. I want to grow up and learn so I can live at the beach with Mom.

She says, "All Labs love the beach."

What is the beach?

I sniff the air at the car window. I've never smelled anything like this before. I can't stop my tail from wagging in circles. I'm getting excited. The car stops. I remember my lessons about waiting.

Finally, Mom says, "Out."

I jump out of the car. I love new adventures with Mom. The sand feels tickly on my feet. I wonder how it is as a back scratcher. I flop over and roll in it. It's tickly on my back, too. Mom is laughing. She likes to watch me have fun. She's such a good girl.

Mom has homework from Mette. We practice new lessons every day. I am smart so I learn fast. On the beach we practice walking slow, slow, slow. I smell the water. I want to get there fast, fast, fast.

Mom says, "Let's go."

That means I get on her left side to practice more walking. I want to raise my head and sniff the air for wild and strange scents to roll on.

Finally Mom says, "Release," and I can play.

I check out the water. It's coming and going. Do I dare wade in? It's not like the lake. I back up and sniff for awhile. What happened? I'm all wet! Ick! Even my head is wet. I hate it when my head is wet. The taste in my mouth is salty. I spit it out. I watch the waves a while. I like the water, but I don't like the waves to crash over my head. I'll watch and jump over them. Mom throws the ball. I'll get it! I'm the best retriever on the beach. I'll jump over the waves and get it. I'll jump over the waves and swim for the ball. This is so much fun. I could do this all day.

Back to work. I'm a little tired from playing, but I need to practice. Practice, practice, practice. Mom needs me to walk on leash and practice the commands right and left so I know which side she wants me to walk on. It's important for me to know how to help Mom. I see a friendly bulldog. He bows to invite me to play.

Yes, I'll play. We run in circles and chase each other. Fun. Oh, no. I forgot about Mom on the other end of the leash. She took a nose-dive into the sand and is lying on the beach, face down, covered with sand. She is screaming. I'm in trouble now. Mom has sand in her mouth, sand in her eyes, sand in her hair, sand in her teeth, and sand down her blouse. What's she going to do now?

Mom grabs me and holds my face. She looks me right in my eyes and says, "Jetta, what a strong girl you are. I don't like eating crunchy sand, so let's go home now. I should have let go of your leash. It's not your fault, Jetta. You are too young to know better. What was I thinking? You are just a silly puppy still."

I want to be a good Service Dog for Mom. I need to grow and learn all my lessons with Mette so I can be with Mom full time on the beach. Oh, happy days! Next time I will do better. I'm a good girl.

CHAPTER 5

First Sleepover

My hips do the hula wiggle when I see my new mom driving up Mette's long driveway. I am nine months old and Mette is letting me go home with Denise for my first weekend visit. I've never before spent a whole day and night with her; I've only had day visits. I stand at the gate with tail wagging and head held high, sniffing the air for her scent. Mom always has yummy treats in her pockets. She smells divine. She is my person to help. When I finish my training, I'll be her Service Dog and I can be with her all the time. Mette taught me to be a good girl, not to jump on Mom and make her fall down. I need to walk very slow with her. I'll try. I'm still a puppy and sometimes I forget.

Here she is! She walks towards me. I want to jump on her and give her my sloppy kisses.

Mette reminds me, "No jumping."

Okay, I'm good. No jumping on new mom. I get to go home with her today. I'm so good and quiet in Mom's car. I close my eyes and next thing I know I'm in my future home.

I see a black cat. Yes, chase that cat.

Denise grabs me and says, " No chase Sara."

I'm bad. The cat ran inside and Mom caught me in the chasing-kitty game. She holds me in kitty-scratching range. Sara hisses at me. Mom makes me stay right there until I stop wanting to chase kitty. I don't like this. Sara could scratch my pretty nose. Denise, please tell Sara that I'm just a silly puppy. Please don't hurt me. I'm in your pack now. Good. She stopped hissing and climbed on her perch to look down at me. She is not happy about having me here. Oh, well. We'll make friends later. I want to get close enough to sniff her all over.

Now Mom says it's time to practice our daily lessons. We are working on "Stay." Easy. I know that one. I am so smart. What a good girl I am. I see a ball coming right at me. Got to get the ball. I'll get it.

Denise says, "No."

I forgot to stay. This is confusing. Oh, I remember now. Mette practiced this with me. Sometimes I get the ball when I wait, but I need to listen for "Release" before I get the ball. Now Mom gets to have fun while training. I hold my head up high and listen. I love learning. I love retrieving. It's my favorite game. I'm such a good girl.

When it's time for bed, I'm tired. Puppies need a lot of sleep. At Mette's ranch, I sleep in my crate in the kennel. Mom lets me sleep in her big bed. Bed is better than crate. I'm housebroken, so Mom trusts me.

While she is sleeping, I slide off the bed to check out this place. I want to take in the smells of my new home. I'm hungry. Maybe I'll find food in the kitchen. I follow my nose. Sara left a couple of tasty morsels. I lick them up. Kitty food is yummy. "Jetta's Vacuum Service" is on the job. I'm still hungry. I taste a kitty brush in the living room. Sharp. Bristles not good. My puppy-teeth want to chew on things. I sniff the handle, then I chew plastic bits of brush everywhere. Different taste, not so good. I taste the TV remote. It's harder than that kitty brush. No taste. I bite down harder. Not interesting. I'll leave some for later.

I should see what is Denise doing. Still sleeping. I'm bored. What is this white roll in the bathroom? I pick it up and take it to my dog nest in the living room. It's soft and easy to bite. What's in the middle? Maybe a treat. Sticky, fluffy stuff gets in my nose and sticks on my tongue. Whee. Fluffy white bits of paper all over the place. Fun.

Denise is calling me. I'm caught in the act. Not to worry, I'm still her good girl. Mom loves being with a puppy. I fill her life. She says puppies need to be puppies, and she will love me forever. Time with her is fun. I will watch her and work hard at my lessons so I can grow up to be her Service Dog. I'm learning. I will be a great helper and get to spend all my days and nights with her. I am such a good Jetta girl.

CHAPTER 6

Farmers' Market Final Exam

Tonight is a big night for me. I've been visiting with my mom so we are meeting Mette at Farmers' Market to see how well I have learned my lessons. I practice, practice, practice, with Mette here all the time, but I haven't been here with my mom yet. I'm only one year old but I learn fast. It's important that I pay attention and help my new mom, Denise. If I don't do well, I can't be with Denise yet, or maybe never. Oh, that's a scary thought. I want to pass this test.

Denise says, "Jetta, let's go."

We cross a big, busy street.

Mom yells, "Slow down!" to the fast cars. Loud cars hurt my ears. Mom is nervous; she doesn't like crossing busy streets at night. Black dogs like me are hard to see. I walk head down, with no looking around. I want to see what all the noise is about, but I am a good girl. I help Mom cross the busy street with honking cars and exhaust fumes. We arrive safely on the sidewalk on the other side where Mette waits for us.

People mill around everywhere. I remember Mette bringing me here for training. Metta says, "Practice, practice, practice." Mom relaxes a little bit now. I smell meat and see people sitting on the curb eating yummy barbecued ribs. We pass by them, right at my eye level. I drool. Mom, did you bring a towel for my slimy slobbers? She knows I can't help it.

We walk up and down in the closed-off street. A lot of people touch me. I am working, so I can't say hello to them. This is hard. A little girl eats an ice cream cone right next to me. I remember ice cream at my birthday party. Maybe I can sneak a lick. Mom, can I at least lick her hand where the cone is dripping on the street? I always hear you say we don't waste food.

"Leave it."

I know what that means, no licking her face or hands. I am a good girl.

We've been walking a long time. Mette says, "Let's sit down and rest awhile." We stop at an outside restaurant.

" Go under," Mom says. I go under the table.

"Go to bed."

I lie down, but how can I sleep now? It's too busy. I can hear Mom and Mette talk about me.

Mom says, "Jetta, stand."

I get up from under the table.

Next she says, "My lap."

That means she wants me to put my feet on her lap and put my face close to her.

"Jetta, kiss." Finally I can kiss her.

"Release." I am off duty.

Mom and Mette are so happy. I passed the test. Happy day. At one year old, I'm on my way to being a professional Service Dog. Mette gives me a shiny gold medallion. It reads "Assistance Dog," and I have my own special number. My practice, practice, practice worked. I am such a good girl.

CHAPTER 7

Canine Good Citizen Test

I see dogs, a lot of dogs, here on the grass with interesting smells. I can tell this is a good dog park. Mom walks me around so I can sniff and do my business. Mette sits on the grass and watches. Today is an important day, and Mom is nervous. If I pass another test, I will be a very good girl, a canine good citizen. I will be even more special than I am now.

We walk towards people waving at me.

Mom says, "Leave it."

I want to wag my tail and greet these people. I am a very good greeter, but not today. We walk in a big circle on the grass.

Mom says, "Jetta, stay."

Easy. I do this all the time. She walks away, across the grass. Wait. I sit here. Heck, I'll lie here. I'm tired from playtime at the beach. Mom wore me out.

Now she says, "Come."

This is too easy. I'll do anything for a treat. Keep them coming. Treats make me drool. Mom knows I'm a drooler and brings towels to wipe my pretty face. Some of the people laugh at my long slobbers, but I can't help them.

Now the people throw tennis balls. I love balls! I'm a very good retriever.

Mom says, "Leave it."

I could get the ball, but I don't because I'm a good girl. Mom praises me. She thinks I'm also a good listener.

What's happening? I can't see Mom and a man is rubbing and touching me all over. Nice man. Good hands. Good rubs. But I wonder where Mom is? I'll sit here and be quiet, but I'm getting a little worried about Mom. He takes me on a little walk. This is fun. I like him. He smells like dogs. I could sniff him for hours. Oh, good. I see Mom. She's back. I do the wiggy-waggy to say "Hi. I'm happy to see you. I've been enjoying this man's rubs."

The nice man says I am perfect for a Service Dog or Therapy Dog. I passed the test. I get a medal for my collar so everyone will see that I am a "Canine Good Citizen." Mom and Mette smile. I am such a good girl.

CHAPTER 8

Visit to Luke

Mom is happy because she gets to take me alone on my very first road trip. Mette told me to be extra good. Mom depends on me to keep her safe. Mette said if this trip goes well, I can be with Mom full time and finish my other training with her. Mom tells me that I am a good girl and she knows I'll be good on the trip. I'm still a puppy, but I am a Service Dog. I'm special.

After riding in the car a long, long time, Mom stops for me to stretch my legs. I'm on a long leash because Mom can't walk where the ground is uneven. I see a running cat. Got to chase. I feel like a wild Jetta. Fun. Mom is calling me. Oh no. I forgot. Am I in trouble or what? I slink back to the car and I give her my most pitiful look. I drop my head and tail to let her know how sorry I am. All is forgiven. I get in the car and we go on our way to visit Mom's son, Matt, and Luke, his dog.

When I get out of the car at their house, I see a handsome Golden Retriever. Luke is so handsome and he is all over me. The dog is a kissing fool, my first love. We are the same age and he loves me, too. We kiss and hang out together. Sometimes he shows a little too much affection. Get a grip, Luke. And sometimes he plays too rough. I hate my ears being bit. Mom says he's a busy, busy boy. No, Luke, leave my toys alone. I draw the line about my toys and bones. I'll just ignore him if I can. He's fun to play with, but he bugs me when he acts like a brat.

Mom takes me on a walk around the neighborhood. Mom likes it here. There are nice trees. I smell rabbits and wild turkeys and squirrels. Luke can't come with us unless Matt walks him because he pulls and jumps to play. Luke could hurt Mom if she tried to walk him. I am trained to walk slow, slow for Mom. Later Matt takes us to the lake where Luke and I are both good retrievers.

Back at Matt's house, Mom opens the gate and Luke bolts out of sight. Maybe it's a fun game. Okay, I'll play with you, Luke. I like chase games. I'll go the other direction to see what happens. Sorry, Mom; I can't help myself.

Run, run, run. I love running. Oh no, I'm tired and I don't know where I am. I haven't figured out the lay of the land yet. Where's Matt's house? It's not to be found. I am hot and thirsty and tired and hungry from running. I see a house with the front door open. Maybe they have food. I walk into the house and wiggle and do my hula dance greeting that gets them every time.

A nice lady gives me a cool drink and says, "Where did you come from? Aren't you a good girl."

I wish I could answer her. I'm so lost. She reads my collar.

"I see your name is Jetta and you are far from home." She calls someone. I rest. I'm hot and tired. I miss Mom. How can I find her again? I'm still a silly one-and-a-half-year-old puppy.

The nice lady walks me outside to see if I remember where Matt's house is. It could be down that circle of houses, or maybe that other direction. I ran so fast for the run-a-way game with Luke that I forgot. I raise my head, sniffing the air. No scent of Matt or Mom. I hear Mom's car coming down the street. My ears perk up. I stand at attention. Matt is driving and Luke and Mom are in the car. Luke's head and shoulders hang out of the car window. He is trying to sniff me out. The car stops and Mom gets out. I wiggle with excitement. Mom is so happy to find me. Luke kisses me when I get in the car. Matt to the rescue. I love Matt. He is a good boy.

Matt and Luke love to play run-away-dog. Mom does not like this game. She gets scared of losing me because I am irreplaceable to her. Okay, Mom, I'll try to be a good girl and not play the run-a-way game. Luke is just a one-and-a-half-year-old puppy. He forgot Matt and his new wife, Jennifer, would be sad without him. Jennifer smells so good and her teenager, Jeremy, plays catch, goes running, and swims in the pool with Luke. Silly Luke forgot his most important new job, taking care of Matt's children, Hudson and Rylie. Luke is a good boy, too.

CHAPTER 9

Bath Time

Oh no, bath time. I hate bath time. I rolled on my favorite carcass at the beach again, and Mom is angry. She says I can't be a good Service Dog when I am a filthy wild thing. She has to go to physical therapy and needs me to help her walk into the building, but I want to be a stinky beast. Mom goes crazy with that hose. I don't like cold water. I'll stand right here, and I won't let her grab me. Oh, no. She is trying to move my body closer to the garden hose. I'm not moving. There is no way she can carry me; she's not strong enough. I'm a dog. I love being stinky.

Where's Mom's friend, David, when I need him? He hooks up the hose to the warm water in the garage. And he never blasts my face. I hate blasts of water in my pretty face. Mom is looking at her watch. She is walking into the house. Yeah, I won this battle. I am such a smart filthy dog. What's that in Mom's hand? A hot dog. She does not play fair. I'll move, but only under protest. Okay, she wins. I move next to her and munch that yummy hot dog.

She is one wild mom with that hose. Is she done yet? I have to stand here and let her blast me with the garden hose. This is torture. I'll turn her in to the Dog Police. Now comes that dog shampoo that Mom loves so much. She says it smells heavenly, but I like my stinky-carcass smell better. I can't work in public smelling and looking this way. I am such a good girl that I stand here even though I don't like it. The suds feel tingly on my body.

I brace myself for another round of spraying. Not my face, not my face. I turn my face away. Right cheek. Left cheek. She tricks me to look at her and then sprays water on my pretty face. I won't look at her. I don't trust her. She is one tricky Mommy. She sprays my face. I hate that. Enough already!

Time for the towel game. That makes the torture worth it. Mom gives me the best rubdowns. Dry my head first, please. I can't stand to have my head wet. That's better. I love it when she dries inside my delicate ears. Keep those rubs coming. They feel so good. Now I flop to the ground. I am so happy. Bath time is over and towel-massage is fabulously fun.

Where is my treat for being such a good girl through the water torture? Bath time tuckers me out, but I will drag my tired self with Mom to her therapy. I do love to see the people there, but I can't go unless I'm clean. They love to pet me and tell me how beautiful I am. I guess Mom's right. I did need bath time. I'd rather be a stinky girl, but my job comes first. I'm such a good girl.

CHAPTER 10

Lifeguard Jetta

Toes, toes, toes. I have never seen so many wiggly little toes. Mom swims at the college pool for exercise every day. People on lawn chairs line the edge of the pool, and their toes dangle right at my nose level like a tempting buffet. I want to sniff and lick. I'm such a lucky girl. I get to be with Mom while she swims.

Only special Service Dogs like me can be here, no other dogs allowed. All the students love me. I get so much attention. But it's hard for me when I can't visit with everyone until Mom puts me off duty. I must watch so she doesn't fall. I have to walk slowly and nicely.

Mom says, "Leave it."

We pass more toes.

"Leave it."

As we pass the long row of toes, Mom says, "Leave it, leave it, leave it," for all the toes. I'm such a good girl.

What a lot of water! I love walking by all these kids. Walking with Mom is always exciting. My tail goes crazy when kids touch me as we go by. I want to lick them to say "Hi." I'll just do a quick lick. This toe has a ring on it. I must sniff that. Maybe a tiny lick. She won't notice. She's busy talking to the lifeguards. Good, I snuck one in. Sometimes I'm a sneaky girl.

Now I must sit and wait and wait and wait for Mom. I stand guard. Boring. I love watching Mom, but I'm getting tired. She swims lap after lap, and my eyes get heavy. She needs me to watch her. The swim team is coming in. They sit cross-legged in the circle on the concrete, waiting for their coach. I stroll over and do my famous hula-girl wiggle. Maybe they have snacks. These big kids miss their dogs at home, and they give the best bootie rubs ever. I back into the circle so they have to pet me. Group rubs are the best.

Mom has been swimming a long time. She must be tired by now. I know when she is tired that she might get in trouble. I have to take good care of her. I must get back to my job. I think Mom's in trouble. She needs me. What to do? What to do? I hate getting my face wet when I jump in the water. I like to wade in. But there's no time to waste. Mom needs me. I jump in to save her. The water feels nice. I swim toward Mom. I am such a good swimmer. Labrador Retrievers are born to swim. We have webbed feet and a rudder tail. I'll save her. She's at the other end the pool, so I must swim fast. Here I am, Mom! I'm saving you!

Mom looks so surprised to see me in the water. I check her over. She's okay. Mom laughs. Why are the lifeguards laughing? The kids on the chairs are sitting up, watching and laughing, too. I was just doing my job. The lifeguards give me a special shirt and red whistle for my neck. Today I am Lifeguard Jetta. I am such a good girl.

CHAPTER 11

Search for the Perfect Ball

Mom says I am in love with balls. Of course I am. I'm a retriever, the best retriever ever. That's why I am so good at my job. Mom understands and wants to make me happy, so I get to play with balls every day. She says that I work so hard for her that she loves playing ball with me. She is such a good girl.

Tennis balls get icky and slimy with sand at the beach. I don't like to put gooey, muddy balls in my mouth. Sand sticks to my tongue and throat. It gags me.

Mom says, "What to do, what to do? I know. We'll shop for the perfect ball for Jetta girl."

We look at the pet store. No perfect balls there. They are either too big or too small or too hard. Darn. Next we go to a grocery store and look in the pet section.

"Do you have any nice balls for Jetta? She is such a good girl," Mom asks the nice clerk.

He tells her, "No, maybe another store."

We try another store. I get tired climbing in and out of the car, trying to find the perfect ball.

Finally Mom says, "Jetta, there is just one more store that might have your perfect ball. We will look at the big store."

We walk through the sliding doors. I'm careful, Mom. I tuck my tail. What do I smell? Popcorn and hot dogs. I can't help it. I drool. Mom wipes my mouth and begins our search. People are all over me, petting and talking to me.

Mom says, "Release."

Good. It's hard to ignore these nice people, and the children's faces need cleaning. I'm such a good girl.

Mom finds the dog toy section. This is my favorite section in the store. I see golf balls—too little. Those are good for my kitties at home, but not for me. Baseballs—too big. Volley balls—way too big. Beach balls—way, way too big. Racquet balls—getting better.

Mom says, "Too small for big dogs."

But Mom, they are nice and bouncy.

"No, not safe. You could choke."

I worry there is no perfect ball for me. How can that be?

Mom looks over to another wall, and I think she sees something. She walks over and reaches up. Holding a box in her hand, she comes over to me and shows me the box is full of balls. Could there be a perfect ball? She takes one out of the box and throws it to me. I catch it. It feels good in my mouth and bounces just right, too. Yay! Mom found the perfect ball for me, and she is loading her shopping cart with boxes of them. My tail wags in circles; I am so happy. Mom tosses one of the perfect balls to me. I carry it out of the store in my mouth. It feels so good; I don't want to drop it.

Mom says, "Jetta girl, you were so patient waiting for your perfect ball, we are going right home to test them on our beach."

Mom is such a good girl.

CHAPTER 12

Day at the Beach

I love playing on my beach early in the morning with Mom. I am special. As a Service Dog, I have an important job—helping Mom balance by walking on leash right next to her. I also pick up things she drops, and she drops things all the time. I am such a good girl. I am big and strong, so I can help if Mom falls. I stand very still while she gets on her knees and grabs me and pulls herself up. In the mornings, we are beach girls.

Mom says, "A tired dog is a good dog. First things first. Dogs need exercise to stay fit for work."

My off-duty time is fun. Mom throws the ball to me. She says I am ball obsessed. I am a good retriever and a good catcher, too. The other people on the beach love to watch me in action, and I love to show off and hear them say how beautiful I am. I am such a good girl. This clump of seaweed smells interesting. That's my favorite scent. Oh, boy! I see long, wild winter grass. The dew is still on it, so moist and sweet and tender. I love my morning greens. What a treat, good to graze on. I can't pass this up.

I see my friend Candy running onto the beach. She is a sweet little herding dog. She lives on a big ranch outside of town. Her dad is a cowboy. He smells divine. Candy is a retired herding dog, but she still likes to herd. She comes to the beach to herd the sea gulls. She is built for speed. I can't keep up with her. Together we run up the hill to the back patios on the cliffs. Candy shows me all the best places to find food. She shares her feasts with me.

Oh, I smell my favorite back porch where the people leave food scraps for the sea gulls. I can't help it. I have to follow my nose. French toast crumbs. That's my favorite scent. Yummy. Candy's dad whistles for her and off she goes like a good girl. My mom is calling me, too. Oh, no. I know Mom is mad at me. I have to go back to the beach. I don't want to get in more trouble. I will act like I couldn't hear her calling. I'll put my head down and walk slow and try to look sorry. I just couldn't help myself. Mom is smiling. Good. She forgives me. I am a good girl.

Mom needs me to pull her up this sand dune. I am a great, strong pulling dog. What do I see way down the beach? Let me sniff the air. Oh, that's Yaya. This Malamute is one wild puppy. She likes me. When she sees me down on the beach with Mom, she howls so loud to get my attention. She loves to dig big holes in sand, too. We are both very good diggers. Yaya knows where her next-door neighbor leaves cat food out, just waiting for us. Yummy, yummy.

Mom calls me to come. She needs me to help her step over the bank to cross a creek. I stand next to her, and she leans on me to step over the running water. I am a good strong Lab. I love helping Mom. I am so special and such a good girl.

What happened now? Oh, no. She is stuck in the mud and can't move. She is stuck up to her knees. Silly Mom. How does she do all these crazy things? Jetta to the rescue again. Hooray! Oh no. She can't get out of the mud. I better think fast. Let's think. I know, I will step sideways out of the quick-sand and save her. There. I will help her hang onto me, and we can crawl out of the mud together to be on sturdy ground. I stand steady and bear her weight, so she can use me like we practiced. We did it. She's up. Yeah, I rescued my mom. Can we play ball now ?

What do I smell down the beach? A fisherman dumped some fish heads. That's my favorite scent. I don't know if I want to roll in them or eat them. Oh, I can't resist. I have to gobble them up. Oh no. Mom's calling me. I can't stop eating these fish heads; they are terrific. Mom's says that I have to walk on leash for a while because I didn't listen. I guess I was a wild girl again. But I'm still a good girl.

I see my friend Cocoa, bowing to invite me to play with him. I've got to go. He is one handsome Lab, but he can be a bad boy. I just can't resist him. Mom thinks he is a bad influence on me, but he is so much fun. I love running through the creek with

Cocoa, my leash trailing behind me. I feel so wild. I can't help it. We check out the trash cans by the picnic tables for food. Just hamburger wrappers, no meat. Oh, shucks. I love hamburger.

Where's Mom? I must go back to Mom. I see her sitting on the beach, waiting for me. I'll do the slow walk with my head down, and maybe she will forgive me again. Mom needs me to help her stand up. I know what to do; I stand very still like a bench, and let her pull herself up. I am such a good girl.

Hey, Mom. Could we go to the deep end of the creek? We are nearby. I lead the way. Mom comes with me. She is a good girl. She loves to see me swim. Mom's smiling. She knows I was born to swim. I have webbed feet and a long strong tail to steer my beautiful self. I'm in Lab heaven. I'll get out and use Mom as my towel. I put my wet head in her lap and lean and flop on her. Shake, shake. I help Mom to cool off. I am such a good girl.

What is that on the sand? A dead sea gull. Got to roll, got to roll. Oh, no.

Mom tells me, "Leave it."

I know what that means. Darn. I really like that rotten seagull cologne. It's my favorite scent. Maybe next time, when she is not so close to me, I can roll.

I love my beach because it has so many wonderful smells. On the ocean breeze come scents of horse droppings, food scraps, fish heads, carcasses, seaweed, muddy creeks, and other dirty, wet dogs. I sniff the air once more and dream of rolling in my favorite stinky stuff next time. Not today, maybe tomorrow. I am a good girl.

CHAPTER 13

Aquanetics Jetta

Mom brings me to a special pool for her water playtime. She loves the warm water here. She says it's her treat of the week. Mine, too.

I see old people. I love old people. They smell different from young people. They spend more time loving me and give my favorite hip rubs with wet hands. It tickles a little. These old people love to see me trotting down the ramp with my tail wagging like a flag. I hear, "Oh, good girl Jetta is here today." Mom lets me go wild—no leash—so I can play with my ball. I show off my good retrieving skills while she exercises. They tell me what a good retriever I am and how beautiful I am. I love all the attention.

I hold my pretty head up and play while Mom swims. This job could be boring, but playing makes the time go faster. I like to play. My favorite game is to plop the ball in the water, so Mom and other people will throw the ball out on the pool deck for me. Sometimes I pretend to slip into the pool, so I get to swim in the warm water. What a treat. Ocean water gets cold. I like warm water best, just like Mom. The old people like my game. They smile and laugh at Retriever Jetta.

Aunt Wilma comes here, too. Mom calls her Aunt Wilma because she loves her so much. Aunt Wilma brings the best treats for me in her bathrobe pocket. As I pass the row of hanging robes, robes, robes, I find hers. I stop and sniff, sniff, sniff. I sniff those treats out of those robes. I know that robe. I sit and wait right next to the robe with the yummy-smelling pockets for Aunt Wilma to get out of the water. I lean up and get a better sniff. Oh. Those treats make me drool. I'm standing in a puddle of it.

Mom yells from the water, "Jetta, leave it. You're being rude."

But Mom, I didn't get enough breakfast. You must be putting me on a diet again.

She is not getting out of the pool. Okay. I'll play with my ball. But first I have to find Wilma and give her a wet kiss. Where's Eleanor? She gives me balls, balls, balls, so many balls. I never saw that many all together just for me. Aunt Wilma and Eleanor are good girls, too. I see another bathrobe with big pockets. I run over and sniff that robe, too. Do you have treats for a good girl?

Mom says, "Leave it, Jetta. Run, run, run."

Okay, Mom. I run. I like running for the ball. Oh! That man threw a long, high one. I run. I'll get it. Glug, glug. I fell in the deep end of the pool. Mom's freaking out. Teacher Alyssa is watching me. How embarrassing. I can't get out of this pool—no doggie steps. Mom is worried. Everybody is watching. A handsome lifeguard runs over. I love him; sometimes he gives me hip rubs. He gets down on the ground at the edge of the pool.

He says, "I've got you, Jetta girl."

The handsome lifeguard pulls me up out of the water. Out on the pool deck, I shake, shake, shake. My lifeguard is wet, wet, wet, from my shaking. Me, too. I am soaked. Can somebody PLEASE dry my head? I lean against the wall. Where is a carpet or a nice sofa to dry my head on when I need it? Mom always dries inside my ears after swimming. I love that. The towel game feels soooo good. I wish Teacher Alyssa would come closer, so I can dry my wet head on her warm sweat pants.

That dip was refreshing. Everyone claps for the handsome lifeguard. He saved me. I lick his face. Everyone is happy. The old people are getting out of the pool. I have to find Aunt Wilma and her robe. Where are you, Aunt Wilma? I'm here, waiting and hungry. I do tricks for her. She smiles. I love her; she is a good girl. I finally get my treats. Good stuff, those Wilma biscuits. I lick my chops.

Oh, I almost forgot about Mom. I need to stay with her when she gets out of the pool, so she won't fall. Back to work.

Mom says, "Jetta, you are the best good girl today. You made everybody laugh. Let's dry you off. You love the towel game."

CHAPTER 14

Jetta's Great Escape

No collar—I feel free, like a wild thing. Mom takes my collar off at night, so I am more comfortable when I sleep. Mom has been sleeping a long time, and I am getting bored just lying here. I wonder if she left any of her chocolate chip cookies on the kitchen counter? I remember one time long ago I took a bag of her cookies. I ran to the front yard and gobbled them up. They were so good. I wonder if there is any food in the kitchen? No food. Too bad.

I look outside. I will guard my yard. I am such a good guard dog. I see a Poodle coming down the street with his mom and her baby. Oh, it's Louie. I go to my fence to give him a sniff and a couple of wags. I love his mom, Clare. Her baby is so soft. I love sniffing babies. She smells like milk and applesauce. Baby fingers are sticky and so good to lick.

What's this? Who left the gate open? I feel a little scared. I will check things out in the driveway and smell the compost pile across the street. Look, no cars coming. It's safe to cross. I am a good girl. I love sniffing here. It's one of the best-smelling yards in the neighborhood.

Maybe Cinder is in her front yard. She is so sweet. She loves to play chase with me at our beach. No Cinder. Oh, well. I can see the beach just down the street. I'll check it out. It won't take me long. I wonder if that rotting carcass is still on the beach? I love that scent. I should stop at this next street and look for cars. Mom likes it when I am safe. I am a good girl.

I'm down on the beach. Yay! I got here! I see something on the sand. I found a ball! Maybe I can find someone to play catch with me. I see surfers coming out of the water. Maybe they will be good for a couple of throws. I put the ball down at their feet and give them my pitiful nobody-ever-plays-with-me look. It gets them every time. Wow! That's a far toss. I'll show them what a good retriever I am.

I run after all the balls they throw. Where is that one? What happened? Ball-Thief steals my ball every time. I never know when he will appear. One minute I'm playing ball and the next the ball is gone, never to be seen again. He is so sneaky; I can't believe it. I was having fun. That dog is going on my bad-boy list.

Walking down the beach, I see Cocoa, my chocolate Lab friend. He's a bad boy sometimes. He comes down to our beach on his own, but I am a good girl. We found the carcass so I'm going to smell great. We roll together on the wonderful carcass. Now we both smell divine. He wants to play chase with me, but I want to dig. Mom says I am a fabulous digger. People stop to watch me dig.

Digging makes me thirsty and tired. I should start for home. I stop at the street and look in both directions. I am such a good girl. I see Zan, our nice neighbor, with her handsome German Shepherds in her yard. The dark one is a little scary; he is a serious guard dog. Zan's Yorkshire terrier tries to bite my ankles. I don't go in snapping-range of her. I love Zan; she smells great with her five dog smells all on one person. You can't get any better smells than that. I get so excited when I see her that my hips do the hula dance. Zan comes home with me; she wants to be sure I make it home. I see Mom. She is worried and upset because I am irreplaceable to her. Oh, I feel so bad. I must have turned into a wild thing for a while.

CHAPTER 15

Birthday Party

Mom reads my birthday invitation to me. "Come to Jetta's Birthday Party (No gifts.)"

What? No gifts? That would be the saddest birthday ever. Mom, are you crazy? Let them brings gifts if they want to. I'm glad dogs can't read. What will I do with no gifts to tear open with my sharp teeth? No wrapping is safe with them. Even the sticky stuff is no match. I hope the nice people will feel sorry for poor Jetta and bring gifts anyway.

Mom says, "We'll see tomorrow."

All night, I dream of gifts and cake and cut-up hot dogs. No dog can resist those goodies.

The next morning is bright and sunny at my beach. Happy birthday for Jetta! I wish everyday was my birthday. Mom, could you give more parties, please, pretty please? We love company, especially with presents. People like cake. I like cake, but it's not good for dogs. Mom gives cake to the people and hot dogs to the dogs. I wish it could be the other way around. Mom says no. Oh well, I tried. She says I'm still a good girl.

Company is coming through the front gate. Chairs are set up on the grass. The beach is down the steps to a sea wall. Mom's friend Doris brings Abbey, my other Lab friend. They came early to help. She never had a big birthday party; she was left alone until Doris rescued her. Abbey wears a party hat, too. I share because I'm such a good girl. I have my pretty birthday scarf on; I'm ready to party. The first guest to come is Mack, a big, fluffy black dog. He is carrying my gift in his mouth. I'll take that gift, Mack. Michelle, his person, is such a good girl. He runs with her on the beach every day. He is a good boy. I love opening gifts. I stick my nose in the bag, and a stuffed animal squeaks. I'll come back to that one. I'll have to attack it later.

Here comes Aunt Wilma. She's always good for a lot of goodies, pretty collars, and the best biscuits. My mouth waters the moment I see her. And here comes Teacher Diane. I love her horse-dog scent and Hailey, her Golden Retriever. Hailey plays hard and runs circles around all my friends and me. Mom loves her. When we play at the beach, she steals the show.

Mom says, "Hailey is so beautiful and sweet."

More people come through my front gate. I see Peter and my favorite black Labrador, Zeke, the hunky Guide Dog. I try to greet everyone, but I still would like to hang around the kitchen where all the food is. Abbey wants to help; I send her out, so I can guard the food. Abby gets excited and nips a little when she greets and kisses. Mom says she must have a little herding dog in her.

Rosie, my girlfriend, and her mom, Martha, bring a stuffed critter. I love stuffed critters. Rosie is big like me, but yellow. She knows she is beautiful. She is a roller. She rolls on her toys, rolls on sand, and rolls on grass. She digs with me at the beach, too. Rosie runs with me and grabs my ball and runs, runs, runs. Then my lazy self has to get the ball, and the game is on.

All doggy friends get hot dogs to munch on. Emi, Jan's dog, plays ball the whole time. She won't even stop to eat. Boy, that's one serious retriever. Dogs in the yard, dogs in the house, and presents everywhere. I am one happy dog.

All us dogs have been playing happily in the sun when Mom hears growling She's coming over to see what's going on. Who's growling at Jetta's birthday party? It's Colombo, the bulldog. He gets grouchy sometimes. He bit off a hunk of fluff from Theo, the sweet Border collie, so Mom puts Colombo on time-out, away from the happy, friendly dogs. Mom says it's not his fault. He didn't learn to play with other dogs when he was a puppy. I never growl. I'm a good girl.

Neighbor friend Jake is a good boy; but he is a little crazy and runs fast, fast. Cheryl, Jake's mom, wants to give him a job because he is full of energy. Let's get

Jake to lead Ring Around the Roses, leading the other dogs away from the cookies. All dogs love chase games. While he does that, I can sneak into the house and get into those peanut-butter cookies that are making me drool all over the place. Cheryl is yelling at Jake, who got so crazy that he jumped over the fence and ran down to the beach. Good going, Jake. Thanks for your help on getting attention off me. Yum. I love peanut butter.

It gets late and all my friends go home. The birthday is over. I am so tired and full of hot dogs, cake, ice cream, and doggy treats. I can't wait for my next birthday.

CHAPTER 16

Therapy Dog

I 'm all clean and ready to be a Therapy Dog. I see a man waiting in front of the special hospital for broken people. Hi, crooked man! My tail wags my greeting. He is so crooked that he must be old, old, old. He lets me smell his crooked hand on his crooked arm on his crooked body. He has so many different smells. I just want to sit here and sniff him for a while. He likes me. He tells Mom about when he hunted with his black Lab when he was young and strong and straight. I like him. I lick his hand, and he smiles. He is waiting for The Jetta Show. I love doing my tricks for groups. I get treats for my tricks. This is my favorite part of dog therapy.

First, we go to the stage, and Mom talks about Service Dogs. Then I do my stuff. Mom wants more people with special needs to have a Service Dog. She shows the crowd how I help her. Mom gets on the floor.

"Jetta, stand."

I get right next to her. She grabs my shoulders and back, then pulls herself up to standing. They clap. I know I am good.

"Jetta, get the telephone, please."

She brought our phone from home, so I could show off. I look for it and trot across the stage and bring it to her. More clapping.

More tricks. Mom brought my toy basket, food dish, and other things for me to pick up for her.

She says, "Let's play with your stuffed animals now, Jetta."

She throws them all over the stage. I snuggle with the soft furry one. It reminds me of snuggling with my kitties at home. My tail goes in circles when I get excited. Too much fun

I hear Mom say, "Jetta, pick up your toys and put them back in the basket, please."

Okay. What a mess we made. I see treats in her hand. I'll do whatever she wants me to do fast, fast. I'm drooling from the smell already. I pick up a toy and put it back in the basket. Treat. Good. Another toy. Treat. Good. One more and one more. Keep those treats coming. Okay, Mom. We are done.

What's next? I'll bring my food bowl. Maybe she will feed me now. I get my bowl.

Mom says "No, Jetta. I said to get my keys."

Everyone laughs.

"One more time, Jetta. Get my sunglasses. "

I get my bowl again. I thought you said bowl, not sunglasses. I guess all this work makes me hungry. All the people are laughing. I guess I was not listening. I get the sunglasses and keys and water bottle and bring them close to her. I listen better this time. My job, helping Mom, is important.

Next, the broken people get to throw the ball for me. They can't throw far. Thank goodness. All this play makes me hungry. I'll try getting my bowl again. Maybe she will feed hungry Jetta. Enough ball chasing; I want food. I bring my bowl to Mom in the hope that she will feed me dinner. All the people laugh at hungry Jetta. I'm a hungry Therapy Dog. Don't they know I have to keep my strength up to help Mom?

Next, we go to their rooms for my pet therapy time. I love it. I just sit or lie down for belly rubs. Some people get kisses. The patients smile and laugh. I love making them laugh. I sense who needs doggy loving, and I go to them first. Then I work the room for any sad and lonely dog lovers. They are my favorite people. Mom shows me off. I love all the pets and buddy rubs, and we both love helping broken people feel happier. My food clock is telling me it is getting close to dinnertime. My favorite, dinnertime.

Mom says, "Okay, Jetta girl, time to go home and feed you."

Yay! A great way to end my day. Mom, you are such a good girl.

CHAPTER 17

Hershey's Last Goodbye

Hershey is my friend. She is a chocolate Lab; that's why her name is Hershey, like the chocolate candy. We spend a lot of time together at our beach. We love each other. She loves me and she loves Mom, too. She kisses her all the time. That's okay. I share her. I am a good girl. Marilyn, Hershey's mom, loves my mom. They are good friends like Hershey and me.

Hershey is old. She can't walk too far any more, but we love digging together. She is deaf, too, but still has her Lab nose. We love wandering around with our moms and getting our noses full of beach smells. Still happy, Hershey gets in the water every day. She takes special medicine to make her hips feel better. Hershey chases my kitty. She wouldn't hurt kitties; it just helps her to feel young again.

But today, Hershey is sick. Mom is holding my sweet friend in the car. I want to give her more room to move around, so I put my head down and ride very quiet for the trip to our vet. Hershey is shaking and falling. She is so upset. Our vet will help her. The veterinary aides come to the car to carry her into the clinic. Hershey wants to walk in on her own, but she just can't move. We all go inside. We all touch her when the vet gives her medicine to help her relax. We all hold her when the doctor helps her go to heaven. I love her, and I will see her on the other side. Hershey loved her life, and she died with her loved ones all around her.

On this beautiful day, Hershey left her body and went to heaven. I still sense her spirit. She is with us at the beach and at the park. I won't forget her.

CHAPTER 18

Jetta Gets Her Kitty

Mom's old black cat, Sara, doesn't want to play with me. I get bored and want to grab her and snuggle into her little furry face. Sometimes she lets me sniff her but never long enough and never her bottom. My dog friends know the rule for being polite. I guess cats don't care if they are polite.

Mom says, "No chase kitty."

I am a good girl and I don't chase Sara, especially in front of Mom. Sometimes I start pounce-play with Sara. Before I know it, I'm in the doghouse. I can't control myself sometimes, but I am such a good girl that Mom tells me I can get a new kitty of my own. I love furry little creatures. They are interesting, like tiny new-born pups. I love to carry them in my mouth. I clean them up so good. Mom's going to let me pick out my new kitty myself.

Mom's friend, Julie, has millions of kitties that need homes. Mom parks in the driveway, and I'm already interested. I see kitties in the driveway napping in the sun, kitties in the yard, and an old cat on the front porch hissing at me. I'll keep away from that one. Hissing kitty, danger for Jetta. She does not want me here. Quick, let's get into the house.

I sniff the air. I smell cat food. Yummy, yummy. Julie smells divine, too, so many kitty smells on one person. She is such a good girl for rescuing all these kitties. I sniff around her house. Fabulous. My nose is so happy. I am so excited that my tail goes in circles. Mom says our home has enough love to go around for more animals. I love Mom. She is a good girl, too.

Oh boy, this house has kitties everywhere—kitties on the table, kitties on the sofa, kitties on the floor. I want to sniff them all. Kitties lounge on the kitchen counter, sit on top of the refrigerator, and peek out of cages. I want to nudge them with my nose.

Mom says, "Leave it."

But they are all over this place.

Happy day, I'm getting my own kitty. This little black-and-white one likes me. I'm so gentle. His fur is so soft. I give him a nice bath with my tongue. He cries a little when my slobbers get him all wet, but Mom holds him, and dries him off with a towel. I was just getting into cleaning him.

We name him Patch and take him to his new home.

He will love it here. Mom is nutty for kitties. She spoils them. I sit here and guard my new boy while he takes his nap. Patch is in my pack now, and I need to keep him safe. I am such a good girl.

I doze off and dream of kitties—little kitties, big fat kitties, fluffy long hair kitties, and soft short hair kitties. I love them all. I love putting them in my mouth and carrying them around. Mom's other cat does not let me pick her up. I can't help it when I am feeling playful.

It's time to feed Patch that great smelling canned kitty food. Sniffing that food makes me crazy. The aroma calls to me from the other room. I drool so much that I get the floor wet. I have to taste that kitty food, the best part of living with kitties. I love it if Mom spills the little yummy nuggets on the kitchen floor. Then I get to be Jetta's Vacuum Service to the rescue.

I am a good girl and watch over Patch and his food. I wait to sneak in when Mom is not looking. This woman is hard to trick. I love my new kitty. His food smells better than my plain kibble.

Mom says, "Kitty food not good for dogs."

Just one little lick, please. Pretty please? Mom says I am a very good girl, but not to be trusted around kitty food.

Mom gets mad at me when I sneak into the kitchen and gobble up all the cat food in sight. How does she know when I get into the cat food? She must have hearing like a hawk. She somehow knows when she sees the kitty dish wet with my slobbers. I wish I could dry the dish so she wouldn't know. I just become a wild thing.

The kitty food aroma fills the house, and I don't care if I get in trouble. Mom is fast asleep. Now is my chance to gobble up the kitty food in the kitchen. I'll slide off the bed, so I don't wake her. The house is dark and quiet. Down the hallway, creep, creep. I see my kitty food on the kitty stand. This will be tricky. I lean up to get my morsels from heaven without tipping the dish over. My long tongue comes in handy. Yum yum. I only wish there was more.

Oh, no. My tail bumps the kitty stand. Crash! Kitty food every where. I need to clean up the floor before Mom comes in. She's mad. I'm caught in the act. She holds the cat dish and waves it at me. I give her my most sorry look. I'll stand here and pretend I'm frozen in fear. That look works most times. I can't even look at the empty kitty dish. Jetta is so ashamed. I will never do it again. I try to be good, but sometimes hungry Jetta girl takes over!

CHAPTER 19

Cookie Monster

Mom is baking today. I love baking day. I'll be a good girl and lick up all the goodies that drop on the floor. Cleaning up Mom's messes is fun. She doesn't want me underfoot while she is baking, so I hang out just outside the kitchen. I'll be very quiet so I can see what she's doing. These heavenly smells make me drool like a dripping faucet.

I want to lick the sweet cookie dough off the kitchen floor. Mom has some sticky dough on her jeans, too. I'll lick off every morsel. Mom says chocolate is bad for dogs; she doesn't want me to get sick. But the taste of those treats would be worth it. Falling asleep on the kitchen floor, I dream of warm cookies, so good and yummy.

Waking up from my nap, I sniff for the cookies. Where did they go? It's driving me crazy. They're not in the kitchen. I'll check the bedrooms. No, just my sleeping kitties are in there. The living room? No, my nose says there are no cookies here. I'll check outside. Sometimes Mom sells treats to her friends.

Yes. I see a big paper grocery bag on the front porch. I stick my head in the bag to peek. I see cookies wrapped in plastic wrap in a freezer bag. Do I dare pull it out of the grocery bag? Yes, I should; I'm the guard dog here. Inspecting all food is my job. You never know; they could taste terrible.

Mom doesn't want to make her friends sick. It's up to me to make sure they taste yummy. What a good girl I am. I'll take them out of the bag to the front lawn to look at them. They look and smell divine. I gently unwrap one with my teeth to get a better sniff. The sticky stuff on the cookies sticks to my teeth and tongue. Icky. Now I have to lick it off. I'll try just a nibble. Maybe I'll eat just one.

Yummy! I love cookies. Mom won't mind; there are plenty left for her friends. But I can't stop eating them. Maybe just one more to make sure they are good. Yum. Maybe I should eat all the cookies; Mom might forget to feed me one day and she would be so sad if I was hungry.

The cookies were so big that I need a drink of water. I'll sneak back into the kitchen to my water bucket. Where's Mom? Do I dare go in the house with chocolate on my face and breath? If she sees me like this, I'll be in trouble. I'll be so quiet.

I feel funny, like a crazy little puppy again. I bounce on the sofa and run around in circles. Whee! I feel wild. I must do something; I have so much energy. Where are my kitties? I feel like a good chase-kitty game. I can't stay still. I jump on the furniture. I can't help myself. Is there more mischief I can get into? I forgot what it feels like to be bad. I'm bad to the bone. I am having a fun cookie day. Where is that good-girl Jetta?

Oh, no. Mom is coming. I'm caught in the act, and I only got to eat four of her big cookies. She's calling the vet; I'm in big trouble now. The vet says not to worry, but I'll be full of energy for a couple of days from all the sugar and chocolate. It's hard to be a good girl all the time. I couldn't help myself. It's my nature to be hungry. I'll be a good girl again tomorrow.

CHAPTER 20

Jetta's Great Embarrassment

Silly Mom didn't say *better go now* before entering this grocery store. I try to hold my water. I am so housebroken that I have never had an accident. Service dogs are good about our potty time. Let's hope this shopping is one of our quickies. Mom stops at the bread aisle. She puts bread in the cart. Okay, let's get out of here. More shopping? Yes, more shopping. She stops and chats to the nice man about her beautiful Lab. I'm such a good girl.

I give Mom my LOOK. I usually stare at her, and she knows that look. Today she must be brain dead or something. I need to go outside NOW. She is still not getting my message. Next, I give a little whine. Still not getting my hints. What to do? I'm getting really uncomfortable, and I don't know how much longer I can hold it. I whimper because I am getting desperate. I jump up and down. I can't understand why she is not noticing my signals.

Oh no! I can't hold it anymore. I squat in the middle of the aisle and pee. Mom gets my hints now.

She says, "Jetta, I am so, so sorry that I didn't let you have *better go now* time like I was trained to do."

She gets a clerk to clean up my mess. Professionals like me must have perfect manners, but I couldn't help this. Mom's face is red because she is embarrassed In the middle of the aisle, Mom is hugging and kissing me.

"Oh, Jetta, I am so sorry. I promise I will never ever do this again. Please, good girl Jetta, how can I ever make it up to you?"

I know. Mom, just follow me to see our nice friendly butcher with the fabulous yummy-smelling apron. He knows what will make me feel better. Can we bring him home with us wearing his wonderful-smelling apron and boots?

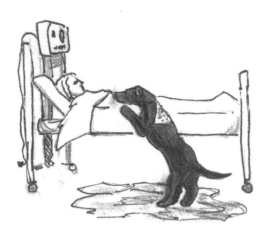

CHAPTER 21

Mom Goes to the Hospital

Mom has to have an operation. We are at a big hospital. I walk next to Mom's wheelchair when she goes into the hospital. People make such a fuss over me and want to pet me. Sorry, I'm in working mode. See my beautiful gold Service Dog scarf? I am on the job. See how good I am?

I put my head down and look ahead, making sure that Mom's okay. I must watch so I don't bump my legs on the wheel. What is in this store with flowers and candy? Mom says it's the hospital gift shop. I want to check it out.

Mom says, "No." The nurses are waiting for her upstairs.

Down the long hallway, I sniff the air for goodies. I'm hungry. What does my nose tell me? Bake sale! I love cookies. I see crumbs under the big table. I'll get them. Tasty. I look for more.

Mom tells me, "No. Leave it."

I'll be a good girl. Darn. Those crumbs under the table are too good to resist. I really have to be good when I'm working. That's the hardest part of my job. I hate leaving crumbs on the floor anywhere. Sorry, Mom. I forgot where I was for a minute. I want to be a good Service Dog.

I see Mojo. He's in training to be a Guide Dog. His puppy handler works in the lab. Mojo is one cute puppy. He is big like me, but still learning his manners. He sniffed me from head to tail. He was so excited to see another dog in the hospital.

I need to be strong today. Mom told me that she has to be away from me for a while. The nice nurses will take good care of her. No! I don't like being away from Mom. She's my person. I don't like it when I can't be with her. She needs me. It's my job to help her get around. I must keep my eyes on her at all times. I feel sad and lonely without her.

Mom is sad not to be with me overnight, too. Her doctor is going to fix her. I love Dr. Yin. She loves dogs. Mom is in a private room, so I can be close to her after the doctor fixes her. I will be a very quiet good girl. Nobody will even know I'm here. I feel better when I can see her. I worry about her when she's out of my sight. The nice nurse is going to take good care of Mom until I can see her again, but I don't want to go home without her. Mom's friend, David, will take care of me when Mom can't. I love him. He plays with me all the time. We have fun together. He will feed me dinner when we get home. Okay, Mom. I'm out of here. My belly is so empty I can feel my backbone.

David takes me home to be with my kitties. The house is lonely without Mom. I miss her. I check the house just in case she's here. No Mom in bedroom. No Mom in bathroom. I'll check her den. Maybe she's in there. No, not there. What will I do without Mom? David is fun. He feeds me treats, and we play ball at the beach until I'm tired, but it's not the same as having Mom. I don't know what to do with myself. I miss having a job.

The next day, David drives me back to the hospital. A nice nurse brings me a cozy blanket. I love it. Right next to me, Mom sleeps after her operation. I must get close to her. I don't want to hurt her; I just want to be there. Mom has something that smells so good. She saved it for me from her breakfast tray. What could it be? I am a good girl. She saved me bacon. What a treat! We never have bacon at home. Full belly, water, cozy bed next to Mom—I'm in dog heaven. I will have happy dreams here in the same room as Mom. We can visit Mojo tomorrow.

CHAPTER 22

Jetta Goes to College

Another school day. Mom loves school. She says it makes her smarter. I like her teacher, Diane. She sees me in the car and says, "Hi, Jetta." She's naughty. Doesn't she see my pretty working scarf? I'm on the job. She forgets people can't speak to me unless Mom says, "Release. "

I listen to Mom's commands when we leave our car. We have to be careful getting out. Parking lots can be dangerous for slow-poke Mom and for black dogs. People aren't expecting to see a dog on campus, and I blend right in to the blacktop.

Mom says, "Out."

I jump out of the car. Oh, no. She just dropped her keys again. She's always dropping things. I am on it, Mom. I pick the keys up, even though I hate metal in my mouth. I do it so Mom doesn't have to bend down in the parking lot. She might lose her balance. Mom, why don't you drop food sometimes? I am a good girl.

The long hallway to her classroom is so narrow that my wagging tail hits both walls. Thud, thud, thud.

Mom says, "Jetta, you have a big tail."

My nose tells me that another dog is here. It must be Zeke, the handsome Guide Dog. We pass in the narrow hallway. I savor every morsel of that male scent. He smells divine. Check out those jowls on that guy. Handsome, handsome. He's usually so serious as he passes me, just a little sniff. But this time, Zeke sneaks a gentle, sweet kiss. He's smart. He knows he would be in big trouble if Peter could see the little lick he gave me. I guess he just couldn't control himself. Zeke knows how beautiful I am. Mom, you go to class and I'll stay with Zeke and sniff him from his head to the tip of his manly tail. Check those jowls on that hunk of a Lab. I'm in love. Mom, can he come home with us, please? He's the one.

Mom says, "Leave it."

Bummer. I listen. I am such a good girl.

Mom is smart; she takes writing lessons from Diane, a horsewoman and a member of The Jetta-Lovers Club. She loves horses and dogs. I smell them on her. Those stable odors are too delicious. I could sniff her for hours. I love napping right under the chalkboard while Mom is in class. There is a saying, "Let sleeping dogs lie." The teacher steps over me like she is used to it. She knows it is rude to interrupt a dog's pleasant dreams. Mom makes me move so Diane won't fall. But Mom, she rides horses all the time. She won't trip over little old me. Mom says that it is very rude not to move for people. But dogs sleep when things get dull. I am such a good girl.

I've been in this classroom for a very long time. I need to go out to the lawn. I give Mom my look that I need to go. Mom tells her friend in the class room, Kate, that my command is *better go now*. Maybe I can sniff Zeke on the way. Down the narrow hallway again, trying to catch up with Zeke-Baby. He walks so fast with Peter that when I am with slow-poke Mom, we can't keep up. Zeke and Peter went that way, Kate, and if we run, maybe we can catch him. Kate knows how to walk a dog. She walks her own Lab every day. I can't find Zeke, but she lets me run, taste grass, and sniff everything in sight. I can smell Kate's handsome Lab on her. We love Kate; she's a good girl.

Back in class, Zeke's smell is already in the room. He is sleeping under Peter's chair. I nap and dream of gorgeous hunk-of-Lab, Zeke. He gives me that one-eye-open look that he does so well. I think he's letting me know that he loves me, too. Zeke is a good boy. I can hardly wait to get him off harness so he can play and do the polite circle sniff.

I hear, "Jetta, get it."

Mom dropped her pen under her desk. A job for me. I pick up her pen and I hear clapping. Her classmates are clapping for me.

Is class over? I give Mom my look. It doesn't work.

Mom says, " Not over yet."

Mom thinks college is fun, but I think it's boring, sitting for so long. Mom is on human time, but I'm on dog time. I whine. I move around a little in my spot. I have had it; enough is enough. I sigh. Then I sigh and yawn at the same time. I yowl.

Diane finally hears me and says, "I hear you, Jetta. It is getting late. We're almost finished ."

Finally, class is over. Oh, for some fresh air and the light of day. Finally outside, I head for the car and hope for beach time. Oh, no. Mom turns around toward that classroom again. No, Mom; we just left. I don't want to go back in that classroom. I'm on strike. Dog abuse! You'll have to drag me. Where is animal rescue when you need them? I won't go back for Teacher Diane, Kate, or even Zeke. Well, maybe for Zeke. I go because I'm a good girl. Thank goodness Mom only forgot her sunglasses. Mom and I are good college girls.

CHAPTER 23

Jetta Goes to Kindergarten

Today is a very special day. I get to go to school and visit all the little people. Mom loves showing how smart and beautiful I am. We pull into the driveway of the school. I see swings, climbing towers, grass, and sand boxes. I love digging in the sand at my beach. Mom, can I dig with the kids? I am a fabulous digger. Please? I see balls on the playground—big balls and small balls. I love balls. I'm a Labrador Retriever; I was born to retrieve. The children are lining up to throw them for me. I can't stop my tail from going in circles when I am so happy, but I don't want to knock the little people down. I would feel sad if they got hurt. I wait for Mom to say, "Release," to raise my head and sniff. I am such a good girl.

Mom says, "Let's go."

That means she needs me on her left side, walking slow. Teacher Jan carries my big toy basket filled with my stuffed critters. I love my toys. Hey, Mom, you should keep your eyes on these children. They like my toys a little too much.

I am going to do tricks for the children later. They wait to take turns walking me. I walk nice and slow in a circle. Easy. Next, I help Mom into the classroom. I see little tables, little chairs, and little children. I am so excited. I smell food at the far end of the room. I have to find a way to get over there without Mom or Teacher Jan noticing. The smell is coming from a row of cubbies where the children store their jackets and lunchboxes. I love lunchboxes. I won't forget where that smell of peanut butter is coming from.

Next, I share my toys. The little girls and boys like my stuffed animals. It's hard to keep track of them. Kids are taking them out of my basket to play with. Some kids want to keep my toys. Mom, send the teacher to get my toys back, please. A little girl is crying. I lick her face. That's okay; I have enough toys. She feels better.

Mom says, "Jetta, put your toys away."

One by one, I find them and put them back in the basket to show the kids how I keep my toys picked up so Mom won't fall over them. The kids clap and want to help me. Good helpers. What fun it can be to pick up toys. But one girl took a toy out. I keep my eyes on her.

The children like to feed me treats. I like the treats from their small hands. The kids are all over me. I am so gentle. I love children. I see a child standing in the corner. She is afraid of me. See my tail wagging? I'm a good girl. The teacher tells us that we can help her not to be afraid.

Mom says, "Jetta, down."

I lie down and put my head next to her. She touches my soft ears and smiles.

Mom says, "Jetta, play dead."

I roll on my back with my feet in the air. All the kids clap for me and say, "Funny Jetta." Mom says I am a good girl.

She shows them the special scarf I wear when I am working. It says *Service Dog*. It is a free pass to go many places other dogs can't. When I wear it, I am on the job. Only Mom can talk to me. My attention must be focused on her needs. She tells the children they must wait until I am off duty to be petted. Even then, they need to ask permission.

Mom tells the children how I help her. I pick up things Mom drops, like keys, sunglasses, forks, pens and papers. I also bring her the telephone or packages the mailman leaves on the porch. If Mom falls down, I stand still so she can use me to help her get up. I guard her and watch over her for safety. My favorite part is loving her and having fun being with her all the time.

Mom tells the children how smart I am. I know forty-five commands. *My lap* means I put my paws in Mom's lap, so she can put my collar and scarf on. *Fix it* tells me I need to untangle my leash, so Mom won't have to bend down. I hear *Leave it* all the time. That means I can't sniff or taste anything I find on the ground. Not fair. There are commands for getting in and out of the car, walking on stairs, and on and on.

Teacher Jan reads to the children about Guide Dogs for blind people, Search and Rescue Dogs, Hearing Dogs for people who can't hear, Therapy Dogs who help cheer up sick people, and Police Dogs who help policemen stay safe and catch bad guys.

Mom and Teacher Jan are busy in the other part of the room. Is this my chance to raise my head and sniff out that heavenly scent of peanut butter in one of those cubbies? The coast is clear. I walk around slowly, pretending I'm just sniffing. I can't help myself; that smell is calling to me. I find it in the last cubbie on the far side of the room. Yep, here is half a peanut butter sandwich, left here just for me. Oh, thank you, wonderful child who left it here. I'd kiss you if I knew who you were.

Mom is calling, and I have peanut butter on my face and on my breath. I am caught in the act. How embarrassing. The whole class is laughing at me. Mom forgives me. Teacher Jan smiles. That child that took one of my stuffed animals is crying and doesn't want to give it back. Call the stuffed animal police. Mom has an idea. The child will give the toy back and we promise to come soon for another visit. Child happy, Mom happy, Teacher Jan happy, full-belly Jetta happy.

Mom says," Good girl, Jetta."

CHAPTER 24

Jetta Meets a Fireman

What has Mom done? She has done some pretty silly things, but this tops them all. I can't believe she crashed into a big, red fire engine. It was standing still, too. What am I going to do with her?

The nice firemen drag her, red face and all, out of our car. They walk her over to a bench and turn back for me. Hi, guys. I guess I'm off duty, so I can wag my tail and get rubs from all these strong hands. Firemen are such good men. But I don't see their spotted dog. I remember seeing a spotted dog in Mom's books for children. The firemen tell me I'm such a good girl.

I raise my head and try to sniff out the spotted pooch. I want to meet him and make friends and do the circle sniff. Maybe I can invite him to play at the beach with us. Working dogs have to play, you know. My nose can't smell a dog here. My nose usually tells me where a dog could be hiding. No, no dog. I forget the dog when the firemen give me hip rubs all around. We should do this more often. They take me to Mom and stand back, looking at Mom's car hooked on the huge fire engine wheel. What to do? What to do?

The fire truck and our car are stuck together. What if there is a fire? What if someone's house is burning? What has Mom done? Here comes the fire chief. He likes dogs. I can tell by the way he smiles at me. He talks to Mom. I see a motorcycle policeman talking to her, too. Chief, where's the spotted dog? When you're finished with the truck, I could use a group rub. What do you think? Too bad there's no dog, but continue these group rubs. I never get group rubs from big, strong handsome men. Mom loves firemen. She says they are heroes. What a sneaky way to meet these handsome men. Mom's upset. It's okay, Mom. See, I still love you. She's a good girl.

Men climb all over the big fire engine. Up close these trucks look so big. They get Mom's car unstuck, and we are free at last. We can go back home to our beach. Driving off after all the excitement, I remember there was no spotted dog. I feel gypped. Too bad Mom didn't crash into a fire truck with a spotted dog. I bet he is a good boy, too. Mom says I was calm and helped her feel safe, but I still can't believe she crashed into a big, red, parked fire truck. So embarrassing. Maybe it's best there was no big, handsome spotted firedog.

Mom asks, "Oh, Jetta. Am I one of those crazy woman drivers?"

That's okay, Mom. I still love you anyway.

CHAPTER 25

Visit to Hansel's and Gretel's House

Pulling up the drive to Grampa and Gramma's, I see my friends Hansel and Gretel. The two littermates stand at the gate. They bark and bark to let me know they are happy to see me. These Weimariners are full of energy, and they are pretty with their sleek, silver-gray fur and big floppy ears. Hansel loves sniffing bottoms. Mom says that is rude. Their tails wiggle instead of wag like my tail. My tail can do damage around coffee tables. Gramma doesn't have to worry with these girls. They have only short tails.

Grampa's sweet Weimariners like me to visit. We make a pack. They even share their dog bed with me. I am a good girl; I wait for them to sniff me from head to paws. Sometimes they hog Mom's time, but I don't get mad. I share Mom. These girls have a lot of land to patrol. I help them guard the front yard when I visit. I am such a good girl.

I see the neighbor cat in Grampa's garden. I'm a fierce guard dog. I chase it off. I feel so wild here in the country. Mom is busy visiting with the neighbors. She won't notice me sneak away. The trash cans down at the end of the driveway call me. Nose alert. I raise my head and sniff. I usually find good stuff there. I jump up and pull one over. Steak bones. Mom never ever gives me steak bones. So good. I tip another trash can over and find something else to eat. Mom will never know what a bad Jetta I've become. Another trash can. Not much food, mostly papers. What a mess I made. I love being wild when I'm off duty in the country.

I see the friendly neighbor and his handsome Golden Retriever, Buddy. He gets so excited when I visit. Buddy's dad has a big fishpond in his yard with big yellow-and-white and gold-and-blue fish. I wonder how they taste? Nose alert. I smell cat food in the open garage. Mom isn't looking. Hungry Jetta needs that cat food. I'm starving. Yummy.

A truck comes up the long drive to Gramma's house. I see a big man with a tall top hat coming up the walkway. The girls go wild. Gramma has to put them out of the room. I like him. He pets me. He smells of chimney smoke. I saw a chimney sweep come to our house once. He's okay. I'm off guard-dog duty. Hansel and Gretel bark and bark. They don't want him here. Gretel tried to bite him. She is the nervous one of the two. The chimney sweep finishes his job and goes into the breakfast room to find Gramma. The back door is open. Gretel goes after him, charging with her head down. She wants to tear him up. Gramma gets the chimney sweep to safety. That was fun to watch.

What's going on with Hansel and Gretel? Afternoon is squirrel-watching time for them. They want to catch that fat squirrel up in the old pine tree. I stand guard with them a while. Hey, girls, that squirrel will never come down with you sitting under the tree. I love to guard the front acreage and chase the neighbor cat off the property. Out in the country, I'm a wild guard dog.

The girls wait for the squirrel, and I look for avocados. This hill has stickers and foxtails that hurt my delicate pads, but I try it anyway. I plow through lots of weeds down the hill. I see an avocado lying on the ground. I take my treat back up the hill to eat on nice soft grass. Oh, no. Mom's calling me. I should go to her. I am a mess. My paws hurt. They are full of awful cockleburs. I limp a little more so I won't get in trouble. I was bad, and Mom's mad, but Gramma is a nurse. She'll take care of me.

It's been a long day in the country. Running around helping and guarding the property is fun, but my belly is empty, and I'm one tired pup. I don't know how the girls do this every day. Gramma gives them canned dog food. They get chunky, smelly stuff for dinner and the biggest biscuits in their crate when they go to bed. Mom never gives me huge biscuits before bed. I just *have* to taste them. Where is everybody? No one in sight or sniffing range. I check out their crates to see if the girls are in bed yet. I'm very quiet. I see two big biscuits in the back. Do I dare go in the crates to check things out? After all, I am in their pack. I sneak in for a taste. I have to crawl in. I'm a good crawler. Mom never gives me huge biscuits. I wonder why? I am such a good girl. I try a nibble. Too good. I have to eat the whole biscuit.

I back up and crawl into the other crate. I'm so sneaky. This biscuit is fabulous, too. Oops. Gramma comes in the room! I am so ashamed of myself. But Gramma smiles.

Mom says, "Oh, Jetta, what did you do? This pup is not to be trusted around food."

She knows that I go a little wild at Grampa and Gramma's house. Mom just blames it on the country. I am such a good girl at home. It's the country and those biscuits that make me to do bad things. I can't help myself. You know dogs came from wolves. Sometimes I just can't resist the call of the wild.

CHAPTER 26

Working Day

Mom needs me to walk with her into the hospital for her physical therapy exercises. Yippee, I get to be the center of attention again. This place is big. We walk through the big sliding doors together. I am careful to be steady so Mom can get her balance. Good. We're safe inside the hospital. I am such a good girl.

Mom says, "Let's go."

That means she wants me to walk on her left side. The waiting room is full of people sitting in chairs and some walking around. I put my head down and go to work. This is my job.

I hear people say, "What a beautiful dog!" and, "Oh, how good she is!" I want to stop and do the hula with my hips and visit with people. I want each person to pet me, but they can't until Mom says, "Release," when I go off duty. This place has a lot of interesting smells, a lot of carpet to sniff, but I can't. I hear the clatter of bottles on a lab tech's tray. I want to stop and check it out, but right now Mom needs me. This hallway is busy—people walking, wheelchairs rolling, a janitor vacuuming. I must guide Mom through without her getting knocked down. I am such a good girl.

I smell food. I am hungry. I like cafeterias. Could we go toward those yummy smells, please? I am a good girl. No time for that. Shucks, we turned down another hallway away from the yummy smells. Mom stops and talks to a nice man. Can I say, "Hi," too, Mom?

I finally hear, "Release."

I can wag my tail and be my friendly adorable self again and get petted. I wag my tail, sniff, and rub on Dr. Keller to say, "Hi." I smell his dogs on him. He loves dogs. I like the hip massages he gives me. Keep that up and I will flip over and ask for a belly rub.

Mom says, "Let's go."

Oh well, back to work.

Mom tripped and fell to her knees. I will help her. It's my job.

Mom gives the command, "Stand."

I stand right next to her and she grabs me and pulls herself up on her feet again.

"Good stand," Mom says.

I'm a good helper.

Down the hallway Mom stops to say hello to the volunteers and lets me visit with the people in this surgery waiting room. Some of them have snacks. I hear the wrappers. Where there's food, there are crumbs. I find them sprinkled on the carpet. If I'm quick enough to gobble up the crumbs, Mom won't notice. But it's hard to fool her. She just knows. I am one hungry puppy, but back to work. I must get Mom to her therapy safely.

One more stop along way to see my friend, Pat. Coming around the corner, I want to go faster. Mom walks so slow. We see a baby in a stroller. I smell Cheerios. I like Cheerios™. I could help to lick up the dribbles. I 'm a very good vacuum.

Mom says, "No."

I forgot that I am working. What a good listener I am.

At Pat's office door, Mom releases me, and I push the door open with my pretty nose and surprise Pat. She loves me. She brings me gifts and yummy dog treats. Pat smells so good. I could find her anywhere in the whole hospital. She has kitty and doggy smells on her. I check every inch of the office for goodies. Food. I smell food. What do you have for me today, Pat? A ball. I love balls, how did you guess? Mom says we will play later.

Down one more hallway to David's therapy office, then I get to take a long nap. We pass leftover breakfast trays on the floor, right at sniffing level. I love food trays. If I pull too hard, Mom will lose her balance and fall. The hardest part of my job is ignoring food. It's hard when the food smells so good and my mouth gets slobbery. When Mom stayed in the hospital, she gave me bacon from her tray. Bacon. I love bacon.

Mom keeps saying, "Leave it, leave it, leave it."

Okay, Mom, I get it. But I need to wipe my slobber on something. Anything will do—carpet, jeans, furniture, a nurse's clean uniform, anything from anybody. Good. Mom has a napkin for me. I can't be expected to work with slobber running down my pretty chin. Where's that nice nurse with the clean, white uniform when I need to wipe my mouth on something?

I helped Mom walk all the long hallways. I am such a good girl. David sometimes has BIG dog biscuits. I wonder if he'll bring treats for me today. I like David; he has two dogs at home, and he smells divine. He gives the best hip massages and tells me I am a good girl, too. I am so excited I can hardly keep my feet from running. I wish Mom could walk faster.

She says, "Jetta, no pulling."

Mom, could you pretend we are playing on the sand dunes, and you need me to pull you up? I guess not. She stopped walking. Mom is getting mad; I'm not listening.

She says, "Jetta, slow down."

If I don't, Mom could get hurt. This is serious. She is the boss. If I want to go into David's office, I have to walk nice and slow. Finally at his office, Mom releases me. I'm off duty. David has a big biscuit for me! Who said work was no fun?

CHAPTER 27

Halloween Hospital

Mom's friend, David, broke his heart, and Mom is sad and worried. The nice doctors are fixing his heart, so he can come home and play with me again. He plays hide-and-seek in the yard and takes me to the beach. He's a good boy.

This is a big hospital with long, long hallways and many elevators. Mom gets lost trying to find David's room. We pass silly people dressed in crazy clothes. Mom says it is Halloween, the one day of the year you can be somebody else. I remember the humiliation of wearing a grass skirt last year. People loved it when I did my hula dance. Mom says any excuse to have fun is good.

Mom gets nervous going in and out of elevators. Those sliding doors are trouble for her. She moves slowly and worries about me getting hurt. Don't worry, Mom. I am a good listener for the command for getting on the weird moving metal rooms. I watch and jump right in with her.

As we walk the halls, people pass us and say, "What a beautiful dog!" I am such a smart Lab, smart and pretty. Some nice nurses want me to stay with them. They have goodies. I think I should stay here. Could I go off duty for a while? I like getting love and attention.

Mom says, "Leave it."

Too bad I can't stop for some rubs from everyone. That would be heavenly. People in this town are dog crazy. Many Therapy Dogs visit sick people.

Mom says, "Jetta is a Service Dog and a wonderful Therapy Dog, too."

I'm such a good girl.

Mom is happy. The hospital staff said we can keep David company and meet his doctors. A nice nurse put a little bed for us right next to his.

"Cozy," Mom says.

It is small, small, small. I'll try not to hog the small, small bed. I am such a good girl.

Crazy doctors, nurses, cafeteria people are dressed in scary costumes. Some are silly, too silly. Mom, I see a big pink bunny with big bunny ears. And here comes a big monster. Is that a police woman? I see her handcuffs and gun. I love Halloween. Usually I help pass out candy to the children that come trick-or-treating at our house. I love kids and candy.

Mom says we both must get some exercise since we did not play on our beach today. We walk, walk, walk, and even climb stairs together. Fun. We walk and walk. Mom reads signs as we go—North Wing, East Wing, South Wing. We get lost, but I know we will get back eventually. Mom trips and falls in the hallway.

She gives the command, "Stand."

I stand right next to her and she grabs me and pulls herself up.

"Good stand," she says.

That's my job. I'm such a good girl.

It's time for Mom to eat, but first we go outside for *better go now.* I sniff and sniff for a good spot for me to do my business. I see the grassy area, but there is a big crack in the sidewalk.

Mom says, "Stand, Jetta."

I stand still so she can lean on me to get over the big crack. It tickles when she grabs my fur.

Back through the big sliding doors, I move fast and tuck my tail. The cafeteria is a great smelling place. I remember the No Begging rule. Food alert. Does the rule mean even spilt egg and bacon on the floor?

Mom says, "Leave it."

Bummer. I drip slobber.

Mom wipes my mouth and says, "Jetta, I know you are getting your tummy ready for food, but you have to wait for your supper. People food is not good for dogs. I know you can't help it. You are still my good girl even though you embarrass me sometimes in public."

Then Mom says, "Jetta, you have been such a good girl, let's find a place to play catch the ball."

I love Mom. I miss my playtime at our beach. We look for a safe, quiet, out-of-the-way place in the huge hospital. It is getting dark outside. Mom doesn't like to walk alone at night. We walk down one hallway and another and another, looking. Mom pushes open a big sliding door.

"This place will do," she says.

Mom throws the ball, and I retrieve. I am a fabulous retriever. Balls bounce pretty good on these hardwood floors. How about another long one, Mom? I run fast and catch one on the fly, another on the bounce. Let's try a high one. Oops. The ball rolled under a bed in the corner. It's stuck. I can't fit under to get it. Mom is such a good girl. She gets down on the floor to try to get my ball. You can do it, Mom.

Suddenly a bright spotlight shines on us in the darkened storage room. A man in a blue uniform with a gun and a flashlight opens the big sliding doors and comes in, staring at Mom. Is he real or just wearing a Halloween costume? Did we break the rules?

A big, handsome German Shepherd stands next to the officer. The dog's ears and tail point up on alert. Security Officer Larry and his Guard Dog, Rudy, stare at us. Mom, can Rudy play with me? I miss my dog friends at my beach. I bow to see if he would like to do the circle sniff and chase me around this big hospital. I show him I'm a good girl with my flat, wagging tail. Rudy stands at attention, his ears pointing straight up, staring at me. A working dog like me, he is on the job and can't play right now. He is serious, but handsome. Mom is scared. Security Officer Larry gives Mom a warning that all dogs in the hospital must be on a leash. But how can we play? No play on hospital grounds. Mom apologizes, but I don't. At least I got some playtime.

Mom says we need to go check on David. We head back to his room. I lead the way, down hallways and up stairs to the fourth floor. Mom is getting tired. It has been a long day. We find David's floor, I think. Did Mom forget which floor? We go to David's room—no David. I smell babies, a lot of babies. Babies in this room, babies in the next room, babies crying in more rooms, but no David. Oops. Wrong floor.

One more trip outside for *better go now.* It's very late, and Mom is tired, but she knows I need to go before bedtime. Mom drops her scarf and needs me to pick it up for her.

"Good girl, Jetta."

Finally, we smell fresh night air. We go to my spot. Walking back to the hospital, we find the big glass doors closed. We are locked out. Mom didn't wear her coat outside or even bring her cell phone to call for help. It is very dark and cold, and Mom is scared. It's my job to take care of her in this big hospital so late at night. What to do, what to do?

Mom says, "Help, we need to get back into the hospital."

Mom looks through the glass doors and sees Officer Larry and Rudy walking away in the dark hallway.

Mom says, "Jetta, speak, "

I bark and bark to get their attention. What a good boy Rudy is. He'll save us. We are escorted back to David's room to sleep all night on the small, small bed. David gets to go home tomorrow—home to our big, big bed, our kitties, and Mom and me to help him feel better so he will be able to play with me again. I'll help him, too. I'm a very good girl.

CHAPTER 28

Scooter Mom

Mom loves her new scooter. We can go more places together faster this way. I don't have to worry about her falling, but I still need to stay close and listen to keep us safe. She puts my bright yellow Service Dog scarf on so drivers can see me better if it gets dark. Mom says black dogs blend with the shadows and can get hurt. Mom, where do you want me to be? This is so different.

Mom tells me, "Side."

I know what that means. She wants me on her right side to be safe. I listen. I stay close to the scooter. I like this new game.

Mom says, "Wait."

I'm a good listener. We will be crossing a busy street. I wait. I'm such a good girl.

Mom has the leash around her wrist. Crossing busy streets is serious. I feel Mom's tension. She's counting on me.

"Stay close," she says.

We crossed safely. Now what? Mom says it's safe on this dead end road.

"Release."

Thanks, Mom. Finally I can sniff and nibble the nice long clumps of grass as much as I want. I'm off duty.

Wow! That scooter goes fast.

Mom says, "Run-run -run."

Fun, I like to run—but where's my ball? She says that comes later, after I get some exercise. Mom thinks I'm lazy-pazy, but I love running next to the scooter. It's fun. Mom is so happy she can go fast with me now. I hear barking. Up the road is a chain link fence with two fierce guard dogs. Running closer, I see two little dogs. I thought guard dogs had to be big and strong and mean. These dogs look like my stuffed animals at home.

The fence gate is open and the two little dogs are coming into sniffing range. See my wagging tail. I'm a lover, not a fighter. Their tails are wagging, too. Friendly guard dogs! We do the circle sniff and make friends. Charley, a maintenance worker of the place, tell us their names are Nicky and Bandit. They let me explore their territory. When I find Nicky's ball, she shares it. She is a good girl like me. I love Nicky's dad, Charley. He throws the ball for me. I chase it. A food smell stops me in my tracks. I sneak into the maintenance room while Mom is talking to Charley. I see bread and I can't help eating it. All this running is making me hungry. I have to keep my strength up. Is there more? Mom's calling me. She doesn't like me wandering off, following my nose. She sees me swallow the last of the bread. Is Jetta still a good girl? Yes, she is smiling. I am a good girl.

Mom gets back on her scooter and we are ready for more adventure. I like this trail. We go over the wood bridge to the cemetery and dog-walking spot. I love this place. So many dogs come here. The cemetery men leave a water bowl out for me. Mom wants me to run some more. More running. She says I have to run off that big piece of bread. I don't care; it was worth it. I run down to the creek. I follow my nose and smell dogs, skunks, deer, and coyotes. All these wild critters bring out the wild side of me.

I forgot where I left Mom. I see her on the grass. She calls me. She is worried because it's getting dark and we are far from home. It's not safe for us at night crossing the busy street. I keep sniffing. I can't stop smelling the wild critters.

Oh, no! What happened? Mom was coming to get me. I forgot about her and she tipped over in her scooter, like a turtle on its back. She is trapped. I go to her. She is mad. I was bad Jetta. I didn't listen. Mom is upside down on the grass and it's getting dark. What to do? I see a man walking his dog in the distance. Mom tells me to get help. I won't leave her again. I bark and bark as loud as I can to get help for her. The nice man came to help her. Jetta to the rescue. Jetta is a good girl again.

We head home. It's almost dark and Mom is freaking out. She wants to get home. We cross back over the wooden bridge and through the chain link fence of the maintenance yard. Clunk. The scooter dies.

Mom says, "What can we do now, Jetta?"

Mom gets off the dead scooter and starts walking slowly down the road. We won't get home before dark like this. All the workers are gone by now. We are all alone here in this big, open place, and it's scary. Mom is quiet. I sense her worries. I have to help her. It's my job.

My dog ears hear a big truck coming towards us in the darkness. I see the headlights. I run ahead and bark and come back to Mom. The driver stops.

"I've seen you here before. I'm Vince. I'll help you."

A black and white pit bull barks and jumps out of the truck. She is a guard dog, too, but she starts wiggling with excitement to meet me. Her name is Page. She is sweet and a good girl like me. I like making friends. Vince's truck is a crane truck. It lifts the whole scooter into the back and Vince lifts Mom and me into his high truck. It is dark when we get home, just in time for dinner. I worked hard for my kibble today. I'll sleep good tonight. It's all in a working dog's day.

CHAPTER 29

Jetta's Lunch Date

What a busy day. Finally Mom stops for lunch. I like my job. I get to go inside great smelling eating places. Most dogs can't go inside, but I can because I am a Service Dog, I'm special. I help Mom stay safe when she walks.

Mom says, "Get dressed."

I put my head through my working scarf to let people know I am a working dog.

I jump out of the car and we walk into the food place.

"Side."

Mom needs me to be on her right side to go through the door. So many people are inside.

I hear them say, "Oh, what a beautiful boy."

Can't these people see that I'm one gorgeous girl? Somebody petted me when we passed their table. I'm on duty, so I can't stop. I have to listen to Mom and not stop for buddy rubs.

I walk slow and steady so Mom will stay safe. We walk past many tables with yummy food on them. Food. I love food. I can't raise my head and sniff that yummy food while I'm working.

Mom says, "Leave it."

This is hard. The food smell makes my mouth drool. I'm sorry, Mom. I can't help it. The food smells so good. She wipes off my slobbers. Thanks, Mom. I wish I could beg for food.

Mom says, "No begging, go under."

I go under the table and lie down. I am bored. I am a quiet and hungry girl while everyone else in this place eats. Workings dog never beg. I'll just starve and fade away to skin and bones alone under this table. Mom, don't worry about me. Hungry Jetta is a good girl under the table.

CHAPTER 30

Grandpa's Last Goodbye

I know this country road. It leads to Grampa and Gramma's house. I love being a country girl. I get wild here. It must be the country air. I smell critters everywhere. Mom gets mad at me for chasing the neighbor off the property. Golden Buddy lives next door, down the driveway a bit. We visit him when we come to the country. Mom says he is a sweet friend, but I can't be trusted alone any more. One time I snuck over and gobbled all the kitty food in their garage.

Mom got mad and scolded me.

"Bad girl, Jetta."

Hungry Jetta took over. Not good.

Two furious gray guard dogs bark when somebody comes up the long driveway. The girls, Hansel and Gretel, Grampa and Gramma's Weimaraners, chase cats, squirrels and possums. I try to help Hansel and Gretel guard the front where they can't go. I also help Grandpa keep that cat out of the garden. I am a good guard dog.

I greet Gramma with my wagging tail and hula hips. We dogs do the polite circle sniff. The girls don't get out much and they are really happy to see us. Mom thinks the sisters are so cute together. They love Mom, and they share their dog beds with me, but they hog Mom's affection when we visit. I share my mom, but I like it better when it's just the two of us. Gretel is a bottom-sniffer. Mom says that's rude. No manners.

We walk into the den. Grampa is sleeping. Mom says he is very sick.

He wakes up and asks, "Where is Jetta?"

I smell how sick he has been for the last several visits. Grampa says I am a very good girl. I give him soft kisses. One hand rubs my ear so softly. I love Grampa's rubs. I am very gentle. Grampa is so tired and wants to see me one more time.

He touches my head and whispers, "Hi, Jetta. You are a great dog."

Mom is crying now and holding Grampa's hand. She really loves her dad. Her sister, Monica, is here with Gramma. We all sit and watch Grampa. He is tired and weak. He is not hungry or thirsty. He says he is winding down. He likes his wife and daughters to be with him.

While Grampa is sleeping, he passes over to the other side. His body is here, but Grampa is gone. He is at peace now. Mom will miss him every day. We planted his little fig tree in our yard for him. One day Mom will see him again.

She says, " Until that time, be happy every day with our memories of him."

Grampa liked me. He told me what a great dog I am. I liked Grampa too.

CHAPTER 31

Lumps and Bumps

I love my vet, Dr. Truax. He takes good care of me. He knows I am a very special girl. As a working dog, I have an important job keeping my person safe for as long as I can. Mom worries about me.

She says, "Jetta, I am going to take the best care of you that I can so you will be around for a very long time."

I remember the first time she saw me limp—we went right to our doctor. Mom is a good girl.

This time Mom is worried about a little bump on my rump. Dr. Truax told her it is very common for Labs to get bumps as they get age. I am eight years old now. He said not to worry. A nice woman takes me to another room and Dr. Truax takes the little bump off my rump. I am such a good girl. Before I know it, we get to go home, but no running or swimming for one week so the spot on my rump can heal.

No fun for good girl Jetta, boring. No playing in the creek. No running for my ball. I still go everywhere with Mom and she gives me extra hip massages. I love hip massages.

The week passes and before I know it, we are back at my favorite vet. This time Mom is sad and crying. What's up, Mom? I feel fine and ready to play. The doctor said it was a bad bump and I have to stay a whole day. They need to take more off my rump.

The next day, Mom leaves me at the vet's again. She has to go everywhere without me. She is sad because she misses her good girl Jetta.

When Mom comes back to pick me up the next day, I'm embarrassed about my bald spot. "The fur will grow back soon," Mom says, "At least we got that bad cancer out of you. It's best to be careful with the animals we love."

Mom takes good care of me and I take good care of her. We love each other. That's our job. We are both good girls, growing older together.

CHAPTER 32

Mom's Other Job

Dogs, dog, dogs. Mom can't get enough. She says she's never met a dog she doesn't like. She likes big dogs and little dogs, old dogs and young dogs. Fluffy ones, smooth ones, any ones. She likes to kiss them and pet them. She says she likes them more than people.

Mom loves taking care of other people's dogs when they go out of town and can't take them along. I'm lucky. I'm a working Service Dog, so I go everywhere Mom goes. Other dogs can't do that. Dogs miss their family and get sad and lonely, but Mom makes them feel so much better. She loves helping dogs stay healthy and happy. She knows that a tired dog is a happy dog.

Teacher Diane's Golden Retriever, Hailey, steals the show at the beach and everywhere we go.

I hear people say, "What a beautiful dog. She plays like a puppy." One day, when Mom was taking care of Hailey, she didn't want to leave her home alone, so she put one of my Service Dog scarves on her and made her a Service Dog for a day. Hailey went to physical therapy with us. She saw her friend, handsome Guide Dog, Zeke. She ran to see him when he came in the door and wanted to play. I never do that until Mom says, "Release." Hailey didn't know the rules. Mom says she still is a very good girl.

Hailey has a nice cozy bed when she sleeps over. She ought to sleep like a happy full-belly dog with all the great food she gets. I am so jealous. Hailey gets special food that helps her not get sick. Mom cooks for Hailey when she stays with us. The smell in the kitchen drifts all over the house. Even the cats want her food. She gets ground turkey, cooked to perfection. How about a little garlic, Mom, for me. They say garlic keeps the fleas off. Hailey gets cooked broccoli and fresh grated carrots and banana, too. You can leave out the banana, too slimy for my taste. Then Mom mixes it with yummy cooked oatmeal. The smell drifts through the house and makes me drool all over everything. I have to wipe my mouth on something. I use the sofa or the carpet. All I get is boring kibble. This is animal cruelty.

Mom says her friend Martha's Golden-and-Lab mix is a diva, whatever that means. Rosie needs a boost to get in the car and bed.

"That's okay," Mom says. "Jetta and I both need a boost at times, too."

Mom takes Rosie to play at the beach with us. She gets the ball and runs fast so lazy me, I have to run after her. Mom likes me to get plenty of exercise. Rosie can get on the furniture and do anything that she wants to do at our house. She's a rolling fool. She rolls on her toys and my ball. She rolls on sand and seaweed, too, but not dead things. Her mom does not want a stinky, smelly dog.

Rosie sleeps with us and one of my kitties on our big bed. She snuggles with Mom next to her and my kitty sleeps by her feet. I sleep on the left side below Rosie. I'm not much of snuggler. Rosie forgets to be lonely when she is here with us.

Rosie gets fed like a princess. She gets yummy canned food that smells like hunks of tender meat. Meat. I love meat. And she only drinks bottled water. And she gets fed in another room, so the kitties don't steal her food. Rosie is afraid of mean kitties. My kitties jump on the kitchen counter and steal meat right out of the can when Mom turns her back. They cry out for Rosie's meat. I drool over her chunky, meaty, delicious delight. And all I get is boring kibble.

Abbey looks like me, only a little bit smaller. Doris, Mom's friend, goes far, far away for her job, so we spend the most time with Abbey. Mom keeps her bed, blanket and food all the time so Doris won't worry about those things when she is far away. We share our cozy dog beds and toys. We are good girls.

Abbey likes to be with people she loves. Doris rescued her from the pound. She stayed in that sad place for a very long time. She was fat and very depressed. Now Abby is one happy dog and she loves Doris. Abbey hates to be left alone. Mom makes sure she has fun every day. We are best friends. We walk our beach and sniff and sniff for food. We find good food, too—French bread, old steak bones, pizza. One time we shared. Sometimes we play chase. Abbey gets wild when we play in the creek. She jumps and bites my delicate ears. I hate that.

We play with toys in the house together. After beach playtime, we get marrow bones. Our friendly butcher boyfriend gets them for us. We love him. Abbey eats when I do, but she gets different food from mine. I like to smell her food dish and Abbey sniffs and licks mine. All I get is my boring kibble.

Sammy is a different story. Mom says he reminds her of Buffy, her little dog that she had a long time ago. She was a little ball of white fluff, too. Sammy missed his dad the first day he visited. He cried and cried. The next time he came to visit, Mom and David played and played with him and he forgot to be upset. Mom knows all about dogs. Squeaky toys are Sammy's favorite, so she keeps a lot of toys in our house. He goes crazy for all my stuffed animals and squeaky toys. He is one wild boy. He chases my kitties. The cats hate him. Mom says he's learning *no chase kitties.* I'll protect them. I am a very good girl.

Sammy sleeps on one of his dad's jackets on top of our big bed next to Mom. He is more of a cuddler than I am. My kitties don't like it much, but Mom says he won't hurt our kitties. He just needs to stay overnight for a couple nights and the kitties will get over it. I don't think so. Topaz gives him looks that scare me, and she is my kitty. Sammy boy, you don't know what you're doing, little cute, white fluff ball.

Sammy isn't much of an eater. I don't understand turning down food. I'd like to try some of his wet canned food. I love the smell. It drives me crazy. Here comes the drool factory. Mom, watch out for a wet floor in the kitchen again. I'd love some of that yummy food. And all I get is my boring kibble.

"Jetta, these other dogs need my help. You are my best girl always. You protect me and keep me safe. No other dog is like you. Jetta, you made me a better person. You are my heart. I keep you in perfect shape, so we will have a long time together."

Mom gives the best hugs and kisses and buddy rubs. I guess I really don't mind the boring kibble. The vet says it's the best for good Jetta girl. I do get my broccoli and carrots and marrow bones and plenty of beach time and playtime. I think the best part of Mom's other job is that I get to be with her all the time, not just a visit. Mom is happy being around dogs, but I am her special one, the best Lab ever. Mom says her heart is full and she knows that her friends trust her with their precious babies. This makes her happy. She loves watching dogs get reunited with their own pack. My favorite part of her job is when they go home. She is such a good girl.

CHAPTER 33

Jetta's Lazy Pazy Day

Mom is getting out of bed early again. Doesn't she know it's still dark outside? I think there should be a law about how early working dogs have to get up. I yawn and go back to sleep. I was having nice doggy dreams about digging in the sand at our beach and sniffing good-smelling rocks.

Mom says, "Time to get up, Jetta. Are you having a lazy-pazy day?"

She goes into the kitchen and I hear kibble hit my dog bowl. I'm up now. Mom knows I'm always ready for breakfast. My full belly makes me happy. I take a big drink from my water bucket and wipe my face on the carpet and the side of the sofa. I crawl onto my dog bed in the living room and doze off again. Maybe Mom will change her mind and crawl back in bed. More sleep is good. I go back to dream land. Mom gets ready to leave the house now. I pretend I'm sleeping. No, she still wants me to come to her.

"Okay, Jetta. Get dressed."

I slip my head through my collar.

"Good girl, Jetta. Thank you. I know you want to sleep, but Mom needs to exercise."

We are off for our day together. I wonder what we will do first? Beach, I hope. It's just a short ride to our beach. The car stops. Yeah, beach first.

"Jetta, out."

I wait. I am a good, patient waiter. We practice all the time. I slide out of the car.

Mom says what a good girl I am. The sand feels good on my tender feet. Mom has a ball in her pocket. I see it and I want it right now. I bark.

Mom says, "No, Jetta. That's rude. You must have better manners."

I wait. Then we start playing retriever girl. I like Mom's short tosses, easy to get, not too much running. I see a nice man on the beach.

Mom says, "Go meet the friends,"

I love greeting people. He throws the ball far. I stop to watch it. I look at the ball, then I look at Mom and I think, that is so far to run. I don't think so. No, definitely not.

Mom yells, "Jetta, get it."

No, I don't think so.

Mom says, "Jetta, you silly girl, are you having a lazy-pazy day? That's okay, you are still a good girl."

I fetch, carry the ball in, and stop to dig. One paw, two paws, push two paws, one paw, push, push. Mom says I am a fabulous digger. And I am a good girl.

Beach time over? Mom heads back to the car. I stop. I give her my sad look, head down. I stand and stare, like I can't move. Maybe we can stay longer? No. Darn. My job calls. Back to work, Jetta. The car is too high to jump into when I'm so tired, so I stand and think. How I can I do this? Mom could give me a lift? No, of course not. What I was thinking? I help her. I take a running start and I'm in. Nap time. Mom drives. I've been sleeping for awhile and I'm still tired.

Mom says, "Out, Jetta."

I pretend I'm sleeping. I finally got cozy here in the back seat.

Mom says, "Jetta, are you having a lazy-pazy day?"

Oh, no, she's messing with my toenails. I hate that. She knows how to get me moving.

Mom says, "Get dressed."

Okay. I'll lower my head, but she'll have to help me put it on.

Mom says, "Get dressed now."

She means business. She needs me to help to put on my working scarf. Gosh, Mom, the car is so high. Could you help me get in?

"Come, Jetta. You can do it."

I slide out of the car slowly.

People love to see me. In the waiting room at the doctor's office, a nice man with wonderful-smelling shoes gives me belly rubs after Mom puts me "off duty." I never get tired of pats and rubs. That's the best thing about working—being off duty. People give me so much attention.

I go back to work until the doctor is ready to see her. We walk down the hall into the exam room.

Mom says, "Jetta, stay."

Great. Nap time.

Later Mom's ready to leave the building.

"Let's go, Jetta."

Mom is ready to leave, but I just got comfortable. Do I have to go already? I don't move. She calls me again. I still don't move.

She says, "Jetta, you are so lazy-pazy today."

She starts to leave without me.

Hmm. If I'm here, how will I get my dinner? I really like this doctor's room, but I don't know where Mom is going without me. Maybe I'll get up—got to stretch first. I'm coming, Mom. Don't leave me. I'm just having a lazy-pazy day."

CHAPTER 34

When I Am An Old Dog*

When I'm an old dog, I'll retire from my job as a Service Dog. I won't wear my working scarf anymore. I will never take another bath. I will be stinky and never go near that garden hose again. I will roll on carcasses at my beach and keep that aroma as long as I want. Mom will have to hold her nose. When I'm an old dog, I will stay at the beach every day until I am ready to come home. I will never, ever, get my tender toenails clipped. I won't be a good girl or let Mom brush my pretty teeth. I will lock my jaw and pull my face away. No, she will never get my mouth open to brush my teeth again. I hate that.

When I'm an old dog and we go to restaurants, I will crawl under the table to catch food from people-plates. I'll scoot past their legs and laps, going from table to table, following my nose. I won't let Mom grab me to make me stop. Mom doesn't like it when I beg. She says it's bad manners. When I'm an old dog, I will give a beggar-dog look, pretending she never feeds me. I'll drool a stream of slobbers, making a little lake under the table. The waiter will cover the floor with towels, so people don't slip. Mom will be so embarrassed, but she'll just have to get over it.

At home, I will chase all cats and wild critters from my yard. I will bring yucky bones in the house, and chew them on Mom's pretty new carpet. I'll climb up on the sofa without permission and wipe my drooly mouth on the furniture. I will crawl under the covers and be a big lump in the bed. I'll stake out my territory first, before the resident kitties settle in. Mom won't mind. She is such a good girl. I will lie anywhere I want, even when I'm a wet, filthy girl. I will pick up my kitties by their little scruffy necks and groom them until they're wet and sticky. I will throw them off my cozy dog bed. No cats allowed. Dogs only. I will not share.

When I'm an old dog, every day will be my birthday, Jetta's special party day. I will eat all the cake and ice cream I want. Friends will bring me presents and yummy treats. I'll tear the wrapping off my gifts like a wild dog, and I won't share my toys. I will chase tennis balls and show off my retrieving skills. I'll eat all the dog cookies myself. Paws off, buddies. We will play all day, eating and running at my beach.

When I'm an old dog, I will bite little yappy dogs when they bug me and not be sweet to rude dogs. I will steal cousin Holly's bones, balls or toys. Payback-time for all ball thieves. I'll sniff people from head to toe when I meet them, and I won't listen to Mom when she says, "Leave it." I will jump on people to be friendly and slobber their faces to say "Hi."

When I'm old and my pretty face is all gray, I will still be the most beautiful Labrador Retriever Mom has ever seen. I'll walk slower. That's okay; Mom walks slow, too. I will still charm the people I greet. They will say what a beautiful old girl I am. I will watch them smile when they see me coming. I want to get pleasantly plump, but I don't think Mom will let me. She says that's so bad for old dogs. She wants me around for a long, long time. She's such a good girl.

When I reach my retirement age, I'll have Mom's new puppy-in-training to torment. I'll sniff and sniff and lick and slobber on him everyday. Mom will have to bring a big towel for my slimy slobbers. I'll finally be the alpha dog. We'll be best buddies, but I will teach the puppy bad manners, and Mom will say, "Jetta was such a good girl. This puppy is a handful." When he finishes his training, he will proudly wear my working scarf. I can be lazy-pazy all day, and still be close to Mom. I know he'll take good care of her. There will be enough love to go around.

*Inspired by "When I'm An Old Woman" from *Warning* by Jenny Joseph

Acknowledgements

Thank you, Mother, for urging me to get a college education. I heard your voice and pushed myself to finish college after my brain injury. I love you, Dad, for introducing me to Cayucos. This wonderful community has nurtured me and made my life with Jetta possible. I am grateful for the best neighbors in the world, Dona and Ed Piercefield, who have taken care of me for the last twenty-seven years.

The love and support from my son Matthew helps me continue my journey. My heart has grown larger because of Matthew's beautiful wife, Jennifer, and their adorable children, Hudson and Rylie, who fill my life with joy I have never felt before. Mora Mace, who is the best goddaughter and niece I could hope for, lets me love her as my own child.

I am indebted to Lynn Foley, Jetta's breeder, for giving me Jetta, the best gift ever; to Mette Bryan, dog trainer turned dear friend, who took a chance on us; to Jetta's wonderful veterinarians, Dr. Truax and Dr. Stevens; to Shelley Alshire, my friend, mentor, and school advisor of many years; and to Patti Wilder who made my college years sweeter by her friendship.

Thanks to Diane Halsted who encouraged me in her writing class to take a shot at my dream of finding Jetta's voice for life-changing instruction and guidance. Thank you to my editor, classmate, and friend, Jan Mayfield, for sharing my dream of this book. Thanks to Pat who started the Jetta-Lover Club and to sister Katy who selflessly helped with her computer smarts. Gratitude goes to my friend and tech support, Steve Boyte, and to Isobel Hoffman whose artwork brings *Jetta's Journey* to life.

And thanks to David for keeping me afloat and to Jetta's dog friends for making her life exciting.

Made in the USA
San Bernardino, CA
23 August 2017